The Mindful School

# How to Grade for Learning

## Ken O'Connor

Foreword by Rick Stiggins

SkyLight
Professional
Development

Arlington Heights, Illinois

**The Mindful School: How to Grade for Learning**
Published by SkyLight Professional Development
2626 S. Clearbrook Dr., Arlington Heights, IL 60005
800-348-4474 or 847-290-6600
Fax: 847-290-6609
info@skylightedu.com
http://www.skylightedu.com


Senior Vice President, Product Development: Robin Fogarty
Manager, Product Development: Ela Aktay
Acquisitions Editor: Jean Ward
Editor: Dara Lee Howard
Project Coordinator: Sue Schumer
Book Designer: Bruce Leckie
Cover Designer and Illustrator: Dave Stockman
Production Supervisor: Bob Crump
Proofreader: Catherine Shapiro
Indexer: Candice Cummins Sunseri

ISBN: 1-57517-123-6
LCCCN: 98-61156

2284-V

Item number 1681

Z Y X W V U T S R Q P O N M L K J I H G F E D C
07 06 05 04 03 02 01 00      15 14 13 12 11 10 9 8 7 6 5 4

# Dedication

To my parents, Hugh and the late Lorraine O'Connor, who believed in me in a way that gave me the confidence to be a risk taker and a challenger of the status quo;

To my wife, Marilyn, and my children, Jeremy and Bronwyn, who have provided me with the ongoing support and encouragement that made it possible for me to write this book; and

To the Scarborough Board of Education [Ontario, Canada], which was my wonderful professional "home" for over 20 years. By the time this book is published, it will no longer exist, as it has been merged with five other boards of education to form the Toronto District School Board.

# Contents

# Foreword

Early in our daughter Krissy's third grade school year, she arrived home after school with a paper in her hand and a tear in her eye. She was carrying a "story" she had written. Her assignment was to write about something or someone that she cared about. She gave it to her mom and me with obvious trepidation.

As we read, we found the touching tale of the kitten named Kelly who came to be a part of our family briefly and then had to go home to the farm because of allergies and because she was just too aggressive. Krissy had wanted a kitten so badly and was so sad about losing her special new friend. The story clearly reflected the work of an emergent writer. As unsophisticated as it was, it captured the emotions of the event. It was quite touching. Krissy's six or seven sentences filled about two thirds of the sheet of paper. In the space below the story at the bottom of the sheet there appeared a very big, very red F. So naturally, my wife and I asked why Krissy had been assigned a failing grade.

Her reply triggered some very strong emotions within both of us when Krissy replied with a tear in her eye, "The teacher told us that we were to fill the page and I didn't do that. And so she said I didn't follow directions and I failed. I don't think I'll ever be a good writer anyway . . . ." As our disappointed little writer walked off, my wife and I could only shake our heads in wonder and fury.

We both know and understand that all classroom teachers face immense classroom assessment, record keeping, and communication challenges. We empathized. First, they must establish rigorous but realistic achievement expectations for each student. Then, they must provide opportunities for students to learn to meet those expectations. Next, the teacher must transform those achievement targets into high-quality assessments, in order to determine the level of student success. Finally, the teacher must transform assessment results into accurate information for those who need access to it and communicate that information in a complete, timely, and understandable form to those users.

Each of these steps can be carried out using sound or unsound practices. If teachers use sound practices, students can prosper. If they use unsound practices, students suffer the consequences. In other words, if achievement expectations are inappropriate (e.g., too high or too low) for a student, the learning environment will be counterproductive. If assessments are of poor quality, inaccurate information and poor instructional decisions will follow. When communication procedures fail, students will have great difficulty succeeding academically.

Krissy's teacher made it part way through this gauntlet of challenges. She wanted her students to write well—an important achievement target. She obviously provided her students with opportunities to write, because Krissy had written her story. The assessment could have been of high quality, because she relied on a direct performance assessment of writing proficiency. But from here on, the teaching, assessment, and communication processes clearly broke down.

In this book, Ken O'Connor gives voice to many of the things that went wrong in this case. Although he centers on the process of communicating about student achievement through the use of report card grades, Ken puts the grading process into a larger context. He gives attention to each of the other keys to success. He argues convincingly for an open and honest educational system—a system in which there are no surprises and no excuses. He advocates the careful articulation of appropriate achievement expectations and the unconditional sharing of those targets with students and their families. He demands rigorous achievement standards and accurate ongoing classroom assessments of student success. Finally, Ken spells out concrete procedures for transforming assessment results into grades that communicate in a timely and understandable way.

The practical guidelines offered in this book help teachers design and conduct grading practices that help students feel in control of their own academic success. These guidelines can keep students from feeling that sense of hopelessness that Krissy felt. Every teacher's goal must be to implement grading practices that lead students to feel that they can succeed if they try.

RICK STIGGINS
ASSESSMENT TRAINING INSTITUTE, PORTLAND, OREGON
SEPTEMBER 1998

# Preface

In May 1990, I had the good fortune to attend a train-the-trainer professional workshop given by Rick Stiggins in Toronto. This sparked in me a general interest in assessment and evaluation, but the part of his workshop that really "turned me on" was the part on grading. Since then, I read everything that I could find about grading. I also watched the passage of my own children through the school system. Each of these influences convinced me that what is needed is a practical set of grading guidelines that support learning and that teachers could apply at the classroom level, that is, in their grade books and computer grading programs.

I began to think seriously about guidelines for grading when I became one of three authors of *Assess for Success* for the Ontario Secondary School Teachers' Federation in July 1993. What led to the real development of the guidelines was a journal article, which I read in April 1994 and which I thought was both wrong and internally inconsistent. I wrote to the editor making these criticisms, and she wrote back suggesting I write an article. At first, I ignored this suggestion, but several months later, she sent me the author's response to my criticism and again suggested that I write an article. Twice challenged, I had to respond, so I spent most of my 1994 Christmas vacation writing an article, which appeared in the May 1995 edition of the *NASSP* [National Association of Secondary Schools Principals] *Bulletin*.

Since that time, I have created staff development workshops based on the article. I have presented these workshops many times in schools and at conferences in the United States and Canada. Most of these workshops were well received and, at all of them, I received interesting comments in the session evaluations. These comments convinced me to try to reach a wider audience by turning my article and workshops into a book on grading.

## What's the Purpose of This Book?

Much of what teachers do is because that is the way it was done to them; this is no longer good enough. It is my hope that this book will lead teachers to critically examine their grading practices. Some of the ideas in this book challenge long-held beliefs and practices and create considerable cognitive dissonance. Glickman said, "There are profound questions about current educational practices that need to debated" (quoted in Bailey and McTighe 1996, 119).

The educational journal article titles and quotations on the first page of the Introduction in this book demonstrate clearly that grades and grading are practices that need to be debated. Even though there are many journal articles and book chapters on the topic, grading is an aspect of education that is discussed very little by practitioners. At the annual meetings of the Association of Supervision and Curriculum Development (ASCD) in 1996, 1997, and 1998, only 11 of more than 2,000 sessions mentioned grading in the title or description! It appears that teachers consider grading to be a private activity, thus "guarding [their] practices with the same passion with which one might guard an unedited diary" (Kain 1996, 569).

This book examines the many issues around grading and provides a set of practical guidelines that teachers may use to arrive at grades for their students. Teachers from kindergarten to college can use the ideas in this book to examine and perhaps change their own grading practices, and, even more important, to discuss this complex, confusing, and difficult issue with colleagues.

## How Is This Book Organized?

An introduction sets the big picture for this book and gives readers an opportunity to identify and examine grading practices and the issues that arise from these practices. These practical grading issues lead to the need for guidelines, and eight such guidelines are provided in subsequent chapters. These are practical guidelines, not just broad general principles. They are important to consider as a set, but also each needs to be considered individually, which is done in Chapters 1 through 8. Each of these chapters addresses four questions: What does the guideline look and sound like? What is the purpose of the guideline? What are the key elements of the guideline? What is the bottom line?

At the end of each of these guideline chapters, a reflection activity (What's My Thinking Now?) asks readers to think about the guideline and its importance and meaning to them. One person's reflections on that particular guideline concludes the chapter.

Chapter 9 examines a number of additional grading issues, including the advantages and disadvantages of different grading approaches, grade point average calculation, the use of computer grading programs, how to grade exceptional students, and legal concerns. Chapter 10 examines the broader aspects of communicating student achievement, considering such topics as expanded format reporting, informal communications, and student-involved conferencing. Some conclusions and recommended actions are provided in Chapter 11. A series of appendices—a glossary, a proposed grading policy, a list of references and an extensive resource list—provide additional information for the reader.

## How Can This Book Be Used?

The most important way to use this book is with an open mind; regardless of how many or few years of experience teachers have, they may use this book to critically examine their own practices. Throughout the book, readers are provided with reflection opportunities, which, it is hoped, they will use to engage themselves more thoroughly with the text. Consider creating a journal to record your thoughts in response to the questions that are asked in these reflection activities.

Engaging with the text can be done individually, but it would probably be more beneficial if it were done in groups (e.g., the whole staff of small schools, study groups, department or division groups, etc.). This is particularly important for the detailed analysis of each guideline at the end of Chapters 1 through 8. Remember also, when changing practices, start small; adapt, do not adopt; and work together. When you have finished the book, you are encouraged to complete the overview reflection at the end of Chapter 11. For this book to be of real value, teachers must use it to critically examine and discuss the almost taboo subject of grading. It is hoped that this will lead teachers to use grading practices presented in the eight guidelines. And, to further encourage your interest, here are my top ten readings, which I think will be particularly helpful to you (see Appendix 3, References, or Appendix 4, Additional Resources, for complete citation):

- R. L. Canady and P. R. Hotchkiss, 1989, "It's A Good Score: Just a Bad Grade"

- T. R. Guskey, 1994, "Making the Grade: What Benefits Students"

- S. Kagan, 1995, "Group Grades Miss the Mark"
- A. Kohn, 1994, "Grading: The Issue Is Not How But Why"
- K. O'Connor, 1995, "Guidelines for Grading That Support Learning and Student Success"
- W. Spady, 1991, "Shifting the Grading Paradigm That Pervades Education"
- R. J. Stiggins, 1997, *Student-Centered Classroom Assessment,* 2nd ed.
- G. Wiggins, 1996, "Honesty and Fairness: Toward Better Grading and Reporting"
- S. Willis, 1993, "Are Letter Grades Obsolete?"
- R. G. Wright, 1994, "Success for All: The Median Is the Key"

# Acknowledgments

During the past eight years, I have been on a journey—a journey of learning about assessment and evaluation. This journey has been assisted by many people; it was initiated and supported over the years by Lorna Earl, formerly the Research Director of the Scarborough Board of Education; it was jump-started by attending train-the-trainer workshops given by Rick Stiggins who has continued to nurture my journey by his interest in and encouragement for my work; and it was moved forward by attending workshops given by Kay Burke and Jay McTighe and by the opportunity to learn from professional friendships with Kay and Jay, as well as with Judy Arter, Kathy Busick, Anne Davies, and Nancy McMunn. On an almost daily basis, I was assisted by Marg Daniel and Dennis Gerrard, my colleagues in the Program Department of the Scarborough Board of Education in Ontario, Canada. Other colleagues who helped me greatly include Angela Boyd, Carol Rocks, George Huff, and Peter Lipman. My journey would not have happened without my "bosses," Rollit Goldring, John Reynolds, and John Donofrio, who provided me with advice and opportunities inside and outside Scarborough.

I also benefited greatly from my ongoing collaboration with Damian Cooper of the Halton Board of Education and Dale Midwood of the Frontenac County Board of Education. My understanding of the practical realities of classroom assessment was enhanced by the members of the Evaluation Policy Committee of the Scarborough Board of Education and by many Scarborough administrators and teachers, especially Stella Dasko, Anita Desrosiers, Lesley Dyce, Lynn Lemieux, and Cathy Pickard. Anita, Lesley, and Lynn particularly helped me to understand assessment issues from the K–6 perspective, which is lacking from my professional background. I also gratefully acknowledge the Ontario Secondary School Teachers' Federation, which gave me my first assessment "immersion" opportunity when I was chosen to be one of the authors of *Assess for Success*. People whose work I admire and have learned from include Robert Lynn Canady, Art Costa, Robin Fogarty, Tom Guskey, Alfie Kohn, Spence Rogers, and Grant Wiggins. Last, but not least, I express my appreciation to Rowan Amott and the staff of the Scarborough Board of Education's Professional Library who assisted me greatly finding references to enhance my workshops and my writing.

There are many others I probably should acknowledge, including all those people who attended my workshops. Although I gratefully acknowledge the contributions of all these people, the responsibility for the views expressed in this book is mine and mine alone. The clarity of these views, however, is only partly due to my writing; I must acknowledge the huge contribution of my editor, Dara Lee Howard. It has been a delight to work with her and to see what a professional editor can do to improve the original manuscript.

KEN O'CONNOR
SCARBOROUGH, ONTARIO
SEPTEMBER 1998

# INTRODUCTION

"Our Schools Grappled with Grade Point Politics and Lost." (Ashenfelter 1990)

"Why Any Grades At All, Father?" (Juarez 1996)

"Testing and Grading Practices and Opinions in the Nineties: 1890's or 1990's?" (Frary, Gross, and Weber 1992)

"Grades are not inherently bad. It is their misuse and misinterpretation that is bad." (Guskey 1993, 7)

"Ten Measures Better Than Grading." (Malehorn 1994)

"Researchers and professional organizations encourage teachers to use multiple assessment measures but give little indication of how to incorporate them into a grade for report cards." (Seeley 1994, 4)

"What grades offer is spurious precision, a subjective rating masquerading as an objective assessment." (Kohn 1993b, 201)

"Letter grades have acquired an almost cult-like importance in American schools." (Olson 1995, 23)

"Many common grading practices . . . make it difficult for many youngsters to feel successful in school." (Canady and Hotchkiss 1989, 68)

"I learned . . . that there are reasons, historical reasons why grading exists. But I also learned from history that there are no good reasons, no sound educational ones, anyway, why they should continue to exist." (Kirschenbaum, Napier, and Simon 1971, 73)

# What Grading Terminology Is Needed?

As the titles and quotes about grading show, grading has many concerns. One communication concern is grading terminology. The term *grading* carries different meanings for different people while other words, such as marking, may sometimes mean grading, too. As McTighe and Ferrara stated, "Terms [are] frequently used interchangeably, although they should have distinct meanings" (1995, 11). Discussion of any issue or principle must proceed from a clear understanding of the meaning of the terms being used. In support of this goal, a glossary is provided in Appendix 1. But, at this point, readers need a shared understanding of two critical terms: *grades* (or grading) and *marks* (or marking). These terms are often used interchangeably, although grading is used more frequently in the United States and marking more commonly in Canada.

## Reflecting on . . . Terminology

Ask yourself the following questions:

1. What do you understand by the terms *grades* and *grading?*
2. What do you understand by the terms *marks* and *marking?*
3. Are they the same? Are they different? How?

The problem is that the terms *grades* and *grading* are often used with two meanings. For a meaningful analysis, it is critical to have a clear meaning for each term. In this book, grading and marking are used as follows:

> Grade(s) or grading—the number or letter reported at the end of a period of time as a summary statement of student performance.

> Mark(s) or marking—the number, letter, or score given for any single student test or performance.

Airasian used grading to mean "making a judgment about the quality of a pupil's performance, whether it is performance on a single assessment or performance across many assessments" (1994, 281). In most writings, the context makes clear which meaning is intended. However, this is not always the case, and, when the meaning is not clear, confusion and lack of clarity in analysis and discussion requires that the two activities be distinguished by using separate terms.

Anderson and Wendel defined marks and grades exactly opposite to the definitions used here. They agree though, that defining terms is essential,

SkyLight Training and Publishing Inc

---

What is your reaction to the titles and quotes about grades, on page 1? What do they say about grading? How do you think your colleagues, your students' parents, and your community at large would react to them?

so that "everyone operates under the same assumptions and knows exactly what meanings underlie those assumptions" (1988, 36–37).

Another definition was provided by Kohn, quoting Paul Dressel: "A grade can be regarded only as an inadequate report of an inaccurate judgment by a biased and variable judge of the extent to which a student has attained an undefined level of mastery of an unknown proportion of an indefinite amount of material" (1993b, 201).

# What Is the Context of Grading?

*Breaking Ranks,* the penetrating analysis of secondary schools published by the National Association of Secondary School Principals in 1996, said, "Teachers will integrate assessment into instruction so that assessment does not merely measure students, but becomes part of the learning process itself" (25). This quote eloquently summarizes the shift in thinking about assessment that has occurred since the 1980s and shows that there has developed a different understanding about the learning process and the changes that have taken place in our economic world.

# Constructivist Theories of Learning

One important understanding has been the development of constructivist theories of learning. Constructivism recognizes that learning is a process in which the learner builds personal meaning by adding new understanding to old on the basis of each new experience. This means that "learning is not linear. . . . Instead, learning occurs at a very uneven pace and proceeds in many different directions at once" (Burke 1993, xiv).

Individuals experience meaningful learning when they have the opportunity to process information and relate it to their own experiences. This implies much for how the teaching/learning process takes place in schools.

> Learners should be able to construct meaning for themselves, reflect on the significance of the meaning, and self-assess to determine their own strengths and weaknesses. Integrated curricula, cooperative learning, problem-based learning, and whole language are just a few examples of curricula that help students construct knowledge for themselves. (Burke 1993, xiv)

**Constructivism recognizes that learning is a process in which the learner builds personal meaning by adding new understanding to old on the basis of each new experience.**

Each of these approaches requires more complex assessment than traditional approaches, which emphasize simple scoring of answers or behaviors as right or wrong. More varied approaches to assessment imply that teachers will not always have neat numbers that can be "crunched" and converted into grades. Grading, therefore, also becomes a more complex activity. Teachers need to consider carefully how they will incorporate data from a broader array of assessments into their students' grades. Guidelines presented in this book help teachers do this because they are designed to support varied approaches to learning and to encourage student success, however it is demonstrated.

## Brain-Based Research

The constructivist view of learning has been supported and expanded by what is often called *brain-based research*. This research has demonstrated that the way the brain works is much more complex than was previously acknowledged in theories of learning. Brain research shows that the ability to learn is significantly influenced by coping with emotions and the environment, by teaching the skills of thinking, and by encouraging metacognition (thinking about thinking).

> The classroom environment that best facilitates the full development of the intelligences is sometimes called "brain compatible." For the brain to function fully, it is beneficial for the classroom to provide five elements: trust and belonging, meaningful content, enriched environment, intelligent choices, and adequate time. (Chapman 1993, 9)

Equally then, assessment and grading practices need to be "brain compatible." Brain-compatible assessment results from paying attention to the same elements:

> *Trust and belonging*, which require that students are comfortable when undertaking assessment activities. That is, students need to be in a familiar environment and have had opportunities to practice each assessment type before the real assessment. It has been demonstrated, for example, that, unless they have had an opportunity to practice a high stress activity in an unfamiliar environment, students perform better on the SAT when they do the test in their own classroom rather than in the school gym or cafeteria. Grading can be made brain compatible by using second chance assessment and by using the most recent information. (See Chapter 3.)

> *Meaningful content* and *enriched environment*, which, from an assessment point of view, mean that teachers provide assessment that promotes learning, not just assessment that is easy to score.

**The ability to learn is significantly influenced by coping with emotions and the environment.**

*Intelligent choices* in assessment means that teachers do not require students to demonstrate their achievement in the same way as other students; students have some choice in how they are assessed.

*Adequate time,* which means that students need time to become comfortable with approaches to instruction and assessment that are new to them. It also means that students need sufficient time to be able to demonstrate their knowledge and skills in assessment situations. Students need only be required to perform in strict time-limited assessment situations if time is a critical element of the achievement being assessed. Reflective learners and slow writers often receive lower grades than they deserve as a result of being required to perform in inappropriately time-limited assessments. This issue is addressed in greater detail in Chapter 3.

Each element of brain-compatible assessment requires that teachers be very flexible in their approach to assessment and grading. If they are more flexible, then there will be a greater variety of information to incorporate into their summary judgments. They will need an approach to grading that allows for more than number crunching. The guidelines in this book are designed to help teachers do exactly this.

## Multiple Intelligences

Another very important understanding has come from Gardner's work with the concept of multiple intelligences. In the past, intelligence was seen as a singular entity, relatively fixed and easily measured. Gardner (1983) demonstrated that, rather than one fixed entity, there are at least eight intelligences:

Verbal/linguistic—words, listening, speaking, dialogues, poems

Visual/spatial—images, drawings, doodles, puzzles, visualization

Logical/mathematical—reasoning, facts, sequencing, judging, ranking

Musical/rhythmic—melody, beat, rap, pacing, blues, classical, jingles

Bodily/kinesthetic—activity, try, do, perform, touch, feel, participate

Interpersonal—interact, communicate, charisma, socialize, empathize

Intrapersonal—self, solitude, create, brood, write, dream, set goals

Naturalist—nature, observe, classify, hike, climb, trees, ecosystem

Knowledge of multiple intelligences requires that teachers focus on how smart students are in different ways; the focus is no longer on "how

**Each element of brain-compatible assessment requires that teachers be very flexible in their approach to assessment and grading.**

smart," but "how one is smart." Gardner believes that each person's mix of intelligences produces a unique cognitive profile. Educators want to ensure that every child learns by building on his or her strengths. Teaching to or through each of the intelligences gives students whose strengths have been undervalued in schools far greater opportunity to succeed.

Understanding multiple intelligences also means that teachers use a wide variety of instructional and assessment activities. One of the best ways to acknowledge individual differences is to encourage students to develop portfolios—purposeful collections of their work—that can show strengths, weaknesses, growth, and progress over time. Ways to use multiple intelligences in both instructional and assessment activities are shown in Figure Intro.1. This figure dramatically illustrates the links that can be made and the incredible variety of activities that are available to teachers to promote student success.

**In the past, educators have held a very narrow view of learning and knowledge, and this view now needs to be broadened dramatically.**

Each of these areas of understanding—constructivism, brain-based research, and multiple intelligences—has contributed to the realization that, in the past, educators have held a very narrow view of learning and knowledge and that this view now needs to be broadened dramatically. Teachers, for example, have focused most commonly on only two intelligences, verbal/linguistic and logical/mathematical, to the exclusion of the other six; students whose strengths are in the other intelligences have frequently not done well in school.

## World Economy

The world economy has changed dramatically in the 1990s. Globalization has given unprecedented freedom based on comparative advantage to the flow of capital and jobs between countries. For the developed world, the manufacturing sector has declined and the service or tertiary sector, which requires higher levels of skill and knowledge, has enjoyed a huge increase. Thus, far fewer jobs are available for those who do not complete high school. The sorting function of schools, that is, creating categories of those who leave early and find low skill jobs, those who complete high school, and those who go on to postsecondary education, does not have the value that it did in the past. What schools now have is the orientation and expectation that students will succeed. Educators consider themselves to be in "the success business," ensuring that students have real opportunity available to them and that the economy has sufficient skilled and knowledgeable people to continue to function efficiently and effectively.

# Portfolios Could Include the Following Activities and Assessments from the Multiple Intelligences

| Verbal/ Linguistic | Logical/ Mathematical | Visual/ Spatial | Bodily/ Kinesthetic |
|---|---|---|---|
| • tape recordings of readings<br>• reactions to guest speakers<br>• autobiographies<br>• reactions to films or videos<br>• scripts for radio shows<br>• list of books read<br>• annotated bibliographies | • puzzles<br>• patterns and their relationships<br>• mathematical operations<br>• formulas/abstract symbols<br>• analogies<br>• time lines<br>• Venn diagrams<br>• original word problems | • artwork<br>• photographs<br>• math manipulatives<br>• graphic organizers<br>• posters, charts, graphics, pictures<br>• illustrations<br>• sketches<br>• props for plays<br>• storyboards | • field trips<br>• role playing<br>• learning centers<br>• labs<br>• sports/games<br>• simulations<br>• presentations<br>• dances |

| Musical/ Rhythmic | Interpersonal | Intrapersonal | Naturalist |
|---|---|---|---|
| • background music in class<br>• songs for books, countries, people<br>• raps, jingles, cheers, poems<br>• musical mnemonics<br>• choral readings<br>• tone patterns<br>• music and dance of different cultures<br>• musical symbols | • group videos, films, filmstrips<br>• team computer programs<br>• cooperative task trios<br>• round robins<br>• jigsaws<br>• wraparounds<br>• electronic mail<br>• class and group discussions<br>• group projects<br>• group presentations | • problem-solving strategies<br>• goal setting<br>• reflective logs<br>• divided journals<br>• metacognitive reflections<br>• independent reading time<br>• silent reflections time<br>• self-evaluations | • outdoor education<br>• environmental studies<br>• field trips<br>• photographs of nature<br>• research on ecosystems<br>• debates on environmental issues<br>• poems about nature |

Adapted from K. Burke, R. Fogarty, and S. Belgrad, *The Mindful School: The Portfolio Connection* (Palatine, Ill: IRI/SkyLight Publishing, 1994), 36.

Figure Intro.1

## How Do These Concepts Affect Assessment?

These economic changes, coupled with new understandings about learning, are leading to significant changes in the ways children are taught and the ways in which they are assessed. There has been a move to *authentic learning*—learning that is relevant to students and to the real world—and to *authentic assessment*—assessment that provides students with opportunities to demonstrate what they know, can do, and are like. (See Figure Intro.2 for a graphic illustration of the characteristics of authentic assessment.) These approaches have moved assessment away from emphasis on paper and pencil methods (especially an almost exclusive reliance on multiple choice questions) toward the use of a broader array of assessment methods with an emphasis on performance assessment.

### Reflecting on . . . Current Methods

Use the checklist shown in Figure Intro.3 to identify the assessment methods you use in your classroom.

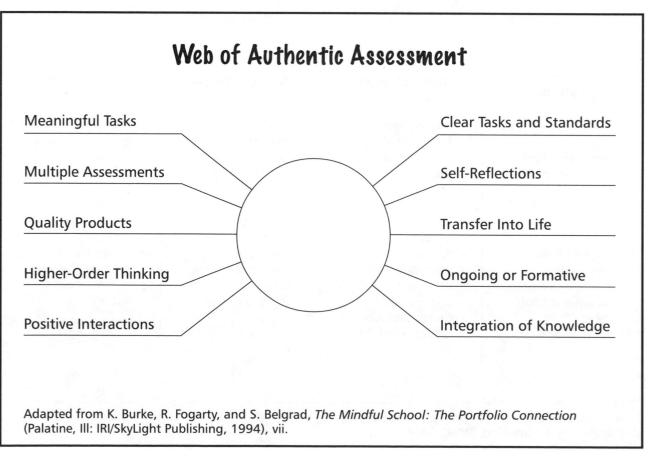

## Web of Authentic Assessment

Meaningful Tasks

Multiple Assessments

Quality Products

Higher-Order Thinking

Positive Interactions

Clear Tasks and Standards

Self-Reflections

Transfer Into Life

Ongoing or Formative

Integration of Knowledge

Adapted from K. Burke, R. Fogarty, and S. Belgrad, *The Mindful School: The Portfolio Connection* (Palatine, Ill: IRI/SkyLight Publishing, 1994), vii.

Figure Intro.2

# Assessment/Evaluation Checklist

## TYPES OF STUDENT ASSESSMENT

### Personal Communication

- ❏ Instructional questions
- ❏ Conferences
- ❏ Questionnaires
- ❏ Response journals
- ❏ Learning logs
- ❏ Oral tests/exams

### Performance Assessment (using rubrics, checklists, rating scales, and anecdotal records)

- ❏ *Written Assignments*
  - ❏ Story
  - ❏ Play
  - ❏ Poem
  - ❏ Paragraph(s)
  - ❏ Essay
  - ❏ Research paper
- ❏ *Demonstrations* (live or tape)
  - ❏ Role play
  - ❏ Debate
  - ❏ Reading
  - ❏ Recital
  - ❏ Retelling
  - ❏ Cooperative group work
- ❏ *Presentations* (live or tape)
  - ❏ Oral
  - ❏ Dance
  - ❏ Visual (photos or video)
- ❏ *Seminars*
- ❏ *Projects*
- ❏ *Portfolios*

### Paper-and-Pencil Tests/Quizzes

- ❏ True/false
- ❏ Matching items
- ❏ Completion items
- ❏ Short answer
- ❏ Visual representation
- ❏ Multiple choice
- ❏ Essay style

Figure Intro.3

SkyLight Training and Publishing Inc

All of these changes and their impact on schools lead to the conclusion that "the primary purpose of classroom assessment [must now be] to inform learning, not to sort and select or justify a grade" (McTighe and Ferrara 1995, 11).

The focus of traditional grading practices is to sort, select, and justify. Traditional grading practices emphasize the use of scores from assessments that are easy to quantify, for example, selected response items, especially multiple choice questions. Teachers "become 'bean counters' . . . adding up all the grades, bonus points, and minus points before using the calculator to divide by the total number of entries—to the second decimal point, of course" (Burke 1993, 140; please note that Burke uses the word *grade* differently than this book). This approach was consistent with the competitive mentality prevalent in schools and society. However, as McTighe and Ferrara suggested, this approach is not compatible with the role grading could play, given what is now understood about the nature of learning and the type(s) of assessment that encourage and support real learning. It is, therefore, necessary to move away from traditional grading and, as much as is possible, use grading in the service of learning. This book provides many suggestions about ways in which grading can be used to inform learning.

## Why Grade?

### Reflecting on . . . Grading Purposes

Reflect on why educators grade students and their work. List as many purposes as you can. When you have finished your list, number each purpose in your order of priority (1 for highest priority).

Through such reflection and with discussion with colleagues, you will find that there are many purposes for grading. To understand this fully, it is helpful to consider classifications from two sources. According to Gronlund and Linn in their classic text, *Measurement and Evaluation in Teaching*, there are four general uses for grading:

- *instructional uses*, to clarify learning goals, indicate students' strengths and weaknesses, inform about students' personal-social development, and contribute to student motivation
- *communicative uses*, to inform parents/guardians about the learning program of the school and how well their children are achieving the intended learning goals

**The primary purpose of classroom assessment [must now be] to inform learning, not to sort and select or justify a grade.**
(McTighe and Ferrara 1995, 11)

- *administrative uses*, to include "determining promotion and graduation, awarding honors, determining athletic eligibility, and reporting to other schools and prospective employers" (Gronlund and Linn 1990, 429)

- *guidance uses*, to help students make their educational and vocational plans realistically (1990, 428-429)

A second source, Guskey, summarized the purposes of grading as follows:

- *Communicate* the achievement status of students to parents and others.

- *Provide information* that students can use for self-evaluation.

- *Select, identify, or group* students for certain educational paths or programs.

- *Provide incentives* to learn.

- *Evaluate* the effectiveness of instructional programs. (1996, 17)

Both of these classifications were developed relative to the broader, double meaning of grading; when the narrower, single meaning of grading employed in this book is used, all of the purposes still apply, although some uses apply more to marks than to grades, for example, self-assessment. Also note that the use of grades, especially traditional grades, for accountability purposes is of very limited value.

It is clear from these two classifications that grades serve many different purposes. Therein lies the basic problem with grades—to serve so many purposes, one letter or number symbol must carry many types of information (achievement, effort, behavior, etc.) in the grade. Putting together such a variety of information makes it very difficult to clearly understand what grades mean. In order to achieve this clarity, a definitive prioritization of the purpose of grades is needed. Bailey and McTighe suggested that "the primary purpose of . . . grades is to *communicate* [emphasis added] student achievement to students, parents, school administrators, post-secondary institutions, and employers" (1996, 120).

Communicating student achievement is the primary purpose of grades. Simply stated, if clear communication does not occur, then none of the other purposes of grades can be effectively carried out. Communication is also the purpose that best fits with what grades are—symbols that summarize performance over a period of time. Communication is most effective when it is clear and concise; grades are certainly concise, and they

> **Communication is the purpose that best fits with what grades are—symbols that summarize performance over time.**

can be clear communication vehicles if there is shared understanding of how they are determined and, thus, what they mean. Instructional and guidance uses not only need to be based on grades with clear meaning, but also are best served by much more information than is provided by symbols. The administrative uses of grades are really a form of communication and are best served when communication is clear. The other purposes of grades are also best served when communication is the focus—clarity about student achievement enables all the participants in the educational endeavor to do what is needed to support learning and encourage success.

Acknowledging that the primary purpose of grades is communication helps to point teachers in some very clear directions concerning the ingredients of grades and the use of grades at different levels within the school system. Emphasizing communication about achievement means that clarity is needed about what achievement is. (See Chapter 1.) This emphasis is reflected in the analysis of grading and the grading guidelines presented in this book.

> **Clarity about student achievement enables all the participants in the educational endeavor to do what is needed to support learning and encourage success.**

# What Are the Underlying Perspectives on Grading?

Seven perspectives, which were developed from a variety of assessment specialists including Stiggins, McTighe, and Guskey, are discussed in the following sections. They provide both a clear indication of the philosophy that underlies the approach to grading advocated in this book and a vehicle for addressing some of the myths about grades and some of the criticisms of grading.

### Reflecting on . . . the Seven Perspectives

Without reading any further, what is your reaction to these seven perspectives? Keep a record of your initial reaction as you read the rest of this section.

1. Grading is not essential for learning.
2. Grading is complicated.
3. Grading is subjective and emotional.
4. Grading is inescapable.
5. Grading has a limited research base.
6. Grading has no single best practice.
7. Grading that is faulty damages students—and teachers.

With which perspectives do you agree? Disagree? Which ones are you not sure about?

## Perspective One: Grading Is Not Essential for Learning

Although many teachers appear from their actions to believe otherwise, "teachers do not need grades or reporting forms to teach well, and students can and do learn well without them" (Guskey 1996, 16). Proof of this can be found in co-curricular activities, such as teams and clubs, and in interest courses, such as night school craft courses. In each of these situations, excellent teaching and superb learning take place—without grades. The problem in the school system is that, as soon as grades are introduced, teachers, parents, and students emphasize grades rather than learning. Teachers usually say this is because grades motivate. Kohn (1993b) believes very strongly that grades should be abolished because as extrinsic motivators, grades destroy positive motivation, which is intrinsic. Kagan, however, suggested that "if a student is performing a behavior and enjoys it and happens to receive praise or recognition, the recognition will not necessarily erode intrinsic motivation" (1994, 16.8). Brookhart offers another view, saying

> . . . Cognitive evaluation theory suggests that if students get feedback that helps them make progress, then motivation and control should increase. . . . Students will behave because their efforts will cause learning, and because enhancing perceived competence is motivating in and of itself. Students will perceive grades and other assessments which teachers use to provide informational feedback as more soundly based and reliable than grades and other assessments used to provide controlling feedback. (1994, 296)

The issue of motivation and learning is of vital importance in this analysis of grading. It is important to acknowledge several facts:

- Teachers need to learn more about motivation so that they can use knowledge rather than perception to guide their practices.

- Students—and parents—have been taught to overvalue grades and, although it will not be easy, if teachers grade better, both may learn to value grades more appropriately.

- Good grades may motivate, but poor grades have no motivational value; in fact, the only grades that do motivate are those that are higher than a student usually receives, or As.

**Students—and parents—have been taught to overvalue grades.**

- Educators must emphasize that learners are responsible for learning. It is then clear that the learner must be motivated by the intrinsic interest and the worth of what is being learned, not by the carrot and stick approach that emphasizes gold stars and A's. Kohn (1993b, 212–221) suggested that what matters is the three Cs of motivation: content (things worth knowing), choice (autonomy in the classroom), and collaboration (learning together).

## Perspective Two: Grading Is Complicated

Much grading is done in a mechanistic way, using formulas to produce the final grade as merely the result of arithmetic calculations. Teachers and students, therefore, come to believe that grading is simple; but, in fact, it is extremely complicated. Grades are shorthand, that is, symbols that represent student performance. In order to arrive at grades, hundreds of decisions have been made along the way; the final grade could be very different if any of those choices had been made differently. In particular, the decisions that are made about how the numbers are "crunched," or manipulated, are critical. This issue is addressed in Chapter 5, with suggestions about how to manipulate numbers in ways that support student learning better than traditional grading practices.

## Perspective Three: Grading Is Subjective and Emotional

Rather than looking at the volume and complexity of the decisions about calculations, this perspective focuses on decisions about what is included in grades and those about the why of calculations. Because grades are usually the result of at least some numerical calculation, teachers often claim that grades are objective measures of student performance; but, as Kohn said, "What grades offer is spurious precision, a subjective rating masquerading as an objective assessment" (1993b, 201). Grades are as much a matter of values as they are of science because, all along the assessment trail, the teacher has made value judgments about what type of assessment to use, what to include and what not to include in each assessment, how the assessment is scored, the actual scoring of the assessment, and why the scores are to be combined in a particular way to arrive at a final grade. Most of these value judgments are professional ones, and this is exactly as it should be; these are the professional

> Teachers and students come to believe that grading is simple; but, in fact, it is extremely complicated.

decisions that teachers are trained (and paid) to make. The basic point here is that it should be acknowledged that these are, for the most part, subjective, not objective, judgments.

It should also be acknowledged that, although most teachers' decisions are based on professional judgment, some are based on emotion. Teaching is and, it is hoped, always will be an interpersonal activity. How we feel about the individuals and the groups being assessed sometimes affects our judgment. Again, the point here is not that this is wrong, but that all involved need to acknowledge that giving and receiving grades is not a purely objective act—it has a significant emotional component. The subjective and emotional aspects of grades have implications for how grading is done; grading will contribute to more effective learning when this perspective is acknowledged rather than denied.

## Perspective Four: Grading Is Inescapable

There are many criticisms that can be made of grades. Willis (1993, 1, 4, 8) listed these:

- Grades are symbols, but what they represent is unclear.
- Grades sort students rather than help them to succeed.
- Grades give little information about student strengths and weaknesses.
- Grades are arbitrary and subjective.
- Grades undermine new teaching practices.
- Grades demoralize students who learn slower.

Many educators believe that grades should be abolished. Although this might be desirable, it simply is not going to happen in the foreseeable future in most educational jurisdictions. In fact, almost everywhere that schools or school systems have tried to remove grades from report cards, they have been faced with community reaction so strongly negative that educators have been forced to return to traditional grades. A clear example of this was described by Olson (1995) in a blow-by-blow description of what happened in Cranston, Rhode Island, when a parent-teacher committee proposed a report card without traditional grades for elementary schools. The committee prepared for the change very thoroughly, including piloting the new report cards. However, when the new format was adopted, the uproar in the community forced the school system to return to the former reporting methods.

**Giving and receiving grades is not a purely objective art.**

Wiggins stated that "trying to get rid of familiar letter grades . . . gets the matter backwards while leading to needless political battles. . . . Parents have reasons to be suspicious of educators who want to tinker with a 120-year-old system they think they understand—even if we know traditional grades are often of questionable worth" (1996, 142). Getting it backwards means that it is inappropriate to focus on trying to eliminate grades; it is more productive to make grades better. Wiggins went on to say that "what critics of grading must understand [is] that the symbol is not the problem; the lack of stable and clear points of reference in using symbols is the problem" (1996, 142). This concern is addressed in Chapters 6 and 8.

Wiggins made another basic point: "grades or numbers, like all symbols, offer efficient ways of summarizing" (1996, 142). Although traditional grades may be of questionable worth, they have a long history. It is not worth fighting against this history; rather, it is worth fighting to make grades meaningful and more supportive of learning. That is what this book is about.

## Perspective Five: Grading Has a Limited Research Base

"What a mass and mess it all was." This is how Middleton (quoted in Guskey 1996, 13) described the literature on grading practices—in 1933! Writing in 1995, Reedy said that "since the introduction of percentage grades in public high schools in the early 1900's, grading and grade reporting have recycled rather than evolved" (47). That there has been no real change over a period of almost 100 years probably stems from the fact that there is relatively little pure research on grading practices. As can be seen from examining the resources in the Reference list (Appendix 3) and the additional resources in Appendix 4, many journal articles and reports have been written on grading, but most of them (as is this book) are summaries of previous work and the opinion(s) of the author(s) on how grading should be done. Logical and well-explained as the articles and reports may be, they do not have the weight or authority provided by research. Teachers freely ignore the advice of authors, even those they acknowledge as experts. Stiggins, Frisbie, and Griswold (1989) identified nineteen grading practices that measurement experts agreed were desirable. When they examined the actual practices of a group of teachers, they found that the expert advice was ignored for eleven of these grading practices. Stiggins et al. suggested three reasons for this situation: recommendations may be opinion or philosophical position rather than estab-

**There has been no real change over a period of almost 100 years . . . on grading practices**

lished fact; recommendations may be unrealistic in actual classroom practice; and recommendations may be outside the knowledge or expertise base of teachers.

Frary, Gross, and Weber came to similar conclusions in their 1992 study and stated that "large proportions of teachers hold opinions and pursue practices contrary to what many measurement specialists would recommend" (2).

## Perspective Six: Grading Has No Single Best Practice

The lack of a research base and the fact that every method of grading has advantages and disadvantages means that there is no one way to grade. The private nature of grading and the dramatic inconsistency in approaches within departments in high schools and colleges and between classrooms in elementary schools means that there are major problems that need to be addressed.

This is especially so where grades are "high stakes," that is, when grades serve as more than communication with students and parents. Thus, when grades are the prime or major component of the decision-making process (e.g., for college admission), there needs to be greater consistency, at least within a school and, one hopes, across a school district. Ideally, there will be principles that could be agreed on and that would lead to consistency across many, or even all, educational jurisdictions. That is the basic purpose behind this book—to provide guidelines that all teachers can follow. Because they are guidelines, not rules, teachers may flexibly adapt them to different grade levels and different subjects.

> **When grades are the prime or major component of the decision-making process there needs to be greater consistency, at least within a school and, one hopes, across a school district.**

## Perspective Seven: Grading That Is Faulty Damages Students—and Teachers

The flush rose on Alan's face. His hands quivered. "It's not fair," he shouted. "I worked hard. I didn't deserve a B+. This will wreck my chances for Harvard." Mr. Beaster stood silent. As Alan took a breath, Beaster interjected, "Alan," he began, "your grade . . . ." Alan glared. "It's not my grade. I worked for an A. I deserve an A. I need it. This is the last semester. The good colleges will look at my grades. If you don't give me an A, my class rank drops." Again Beaster tried to interrupt, but Alan kept on, nostrils flaring, his face now beet-red, "You're cheating me," he screeched. "You're ruining my life. My father will kill me. There's no way this grade is O.K. If you liked me you would give me an A. You're not fair." "Alan," countered Beaster, "I'm not going to debate this grade with you. If you want to discuss it when you're calm, I'll be glad to." "Bull____ . You'll never change it," Alan pouted as he turned to leave. "You teachers are all alike. You ____ ." (Bellanca 1992, 297)

Carmela stared at the floor. Mrs. Martinez sat beside her. Carmela did not move. "Carmela, what am I going to do with you?" Mrs. Martinez asked. "Your grades are getting worse. You are a bright girl. You should be doing better. You are not a D student." Carmela still did not move. "I do care," she thought, "but it's not so easy. It never has been easy. I've got more to think about than school. School doesn't help me make the dinner or watch my brothers and sisters at night—especially when there is no dinner. And even if I do study, I'm always getting a C or D. So why bother? I can do C or D without studying." (Bellanca 1992, 297)

These two stories illustrate some of the problems with traditional grading practices. Alan had no concept of what good work was or how his grades were calculated. He had developed the idea that school was only about grades, not learning, and that teachers "gave" good grades to students they liked rather than those who produced quality work. Carmela had different problems; there were too many other things in her life for her to be able to show her ability by producing quality work on demand. Rather than becoming angry, as Alan did, she developed a sense of the inevitable—whatever she did she would get Cs or Ds, so there was no point in trying to improve.

Overemphasis on grades and faulty grading practices have detrimental effects on student achievement, motivation, and self-concept, as can be seen in these examples. Faulty grading also damages the interpersonal relationship on which good teaching and effective learning depend. This problem occurs at least partly because of teachers' dual roles as coach and judge. Unfortunately, these roles frequently conflict and, as a result, teacher–student relationships are damaged. Many of the problems illustrated by Alan's and Carmela's stories may be at least alleviated and possibly even eliminated if grading practices that support learning and student success are used.

These perspectives on grading contrast with traditional perspectives on grading. Traditional grading is normally seen as being essential for learning ("If I don't give them grades, they won't do the work") and as straightforward and scientific ("The formula says . . .; the calculator shows . . ."). If one followed the first three perspectives to their logical

**Overemphasis on grades and faulty grading practices have detrimental effects on student achievement, motivation, and self-concept.**

conclusion, a strong case could be made against grading; but the fourth perspective means that, as it is virtually impossible to do away with grades, it is necessary to find ways to do them better. Here, better means to develop grading practices that support learning and encourage student success. Teachers must not see grades as weapons of control, but rather use grading as an exercise in professional judgment to enhance learning. If the seven perspectives are acknowledged by teachers in their dealings with parents, students, and other teachers, grades can become a positive rather than a punitive aspect of educational practice.

### Reflecting on . . . the Perspectives

Now that you have read about each of the perspectives, what do you think?

- With which perspectives do you now agree? Disagree?
- Which perspectives in the list are you now not sure about?
- How did your thinking change from when you first read the list?

## Grading Practices, Issues, and Guidelines

This section actively engages readers in analyzing grading practices. It begins with some factual data about grading practices; readers then examine their own beliefs about grading and their own grading practices. Next, seven case studies provide opportunities to analyze grading practices and identify grading issues—the what, how, and why of grading. Readers might keep a list of the issues that they identify to compare with a list provided in the text. Having identified grading issues, one looks for solutions. One solution is practical guidelines that teachers may use in their classrooms and in their gradebooks. A set of eight such guidelines is introduced in this section and examined in detail in Chapters 1 through 8.

## How Is Grading Done?

Robinson and Craver (1989, 26) reported the use of letter and percentage grades at various grade levels in the United States in 1988. Figure Intro.4 shows the usage levels for the two most prevalent grading symbol systems: letters and percentages. Unfortunately, there has been no comparable report in the 1990s.

This information demonstrates that letter or percentage grades were given to 15% to 20% of kindergarten students; 55% to 70% of students in Grades 1–3; and 80% to 100% of students in Grades 4–12.

> **The use of letters or percentage grades is a significant fact of life for most students, parents, and teachers in North America.**

# Percentage of School Districts Reporting Use of Different Grading Symbols at Different Grade Levels[1]

| Grade | Letter | Percentage |
|-------|--------|------------|
| Kindergarten | 14.8% | 4.8% |
| Grades 1–3 | 55.4% | 15.6% |
| Grades 4–6 | 79.2% | 20.7% |
| Grades 7–9 | 81.9% | 26.8% |
| Grades 10–12 | 80.2% | 28.5% |

Data from G. E. Robinson and J. M. Craver, *Assessing and Grading Student Achievement*. (Arlington, Va.: Educational Research Service, 1989), 26.

[1]Percentages may total more than 100% because some districts may use more than one grading symbol system at a grade level.

Figure Intro.4

There is no reason to believe that the proportions have changed dramatically since Robinson and Craver's 1989 report. We are, therefore, examining an educational practice that is a significant fact of life for most students, parents, and teachers in North America.

## How Do YOU Grade?

Guskey said, "[Grading] practices are not the result of careful thought or sound evidence, . . . Rather, they are used because teachers experienced these practices as students and, having little training or experience with other options, continue their use" (1996, 20). This statement may be unfair to some teachers, but it is certainly true for many, maybe even most, teachers.

### Reflecting on . . . Your Grading Practices

1. What are your grading practice principles?

2. What are your actual grading practices? Do you grade on the "curve"?

3. What were or are the main influences on your grading principles and practices?

4. How do your grading principles and practices compare with those of other teachers in your school?

One of the best ways to analyze grading practices (and the principles behind them) is to analyze a set of marks and grades and identify the issues that arise from such an analysis. Following are seven case studies that give us the opportunity to analyze grading practices and discover grading issues. See the margin for reflection questions.

## Case Study 1: Interim Report Card Grade

Case Study 1 considers the impact of a zero mark on a grade and the possible impact on a student of grade reporting very early in a course/year.

The marks in the chart were given to a student in a senior science class on an interim report card in a school with a semestered block schedule after four weeks of 76-minute classes.

| | SCORES | |
|---|---|---|
| Task | Mark/Total Possible | Percentage |
| **Tests (50%)** | | |
| Symbols | 17/20 | 85 |
| Matter | 0/68 (absent) | 0 |
| Reactions | 35.5/46 | 75 |
| **Daily Work (25%)** | | |
| Assignment | 10/10 | 100 |
| Homework | 10/10 | 100 |
| Homework | 9/10 | 90 |
| Atom Quiz | 10/10 | 100 |
| Moles Quiz | 5/8 | 62.5 |
| Homework | omit/10 | omit |
| **Lab Work (25%)** | | |
| MP/BP | 14.5/15 | 96.7 |
| Superation | 20/24 | 83.3 |
| Reactions | 7/10 | 70 |
| Periodicity Check | 10/10 | 100 |

This case study dramatically illustrates the effect of assigning a zero for a missed test. The student has six marks of 90% or higher, two marks in the 80s, and no mark lower than 62.5%; but, the interim grade is lower than the lowest mark! A grade like this could have a devastating effect on students, causing them to give up. This student is achieving well, but the grade suggests otherwise—because of a missed test.

## Case Study 2: Chris Brown's Science Class

Case Study 2 considers the marks and grades of a teacher using a very traditional approach to grading. The student marks have been arranged

**Case Study 1: Reflection**

1. What grade would you give the student? Why?

2. The actual grade the student received was 58.3%. What is your reaction to this grade? Was this grade a fair reflection of the student's overall performance?

3. What grading issues arise from this case study?

**Case Study 2: Reflection**

1. Do the grades awarded fairly reflect the results from which they were derived for each student?

2. If you indicated "yes," for which students? Why?

3. If you indicated "no," for which students? Why?

4. What grading issues arise from this case study?

so that, for most students, there are some obvious problems with their performance and/or the way it is graded.

The marks and grades in the chart are for Chris Brown's science class in Ontario. If you are not a science teacher, put the appropriate items for your subject in place of the lab reports, care of equipment, and so forth. Note carefully the information that is shown below the grade book extract regarding the miscellaneous items, the way absence is dealt with, and the grading scale. Enter to the right of the chart the letter grade each student would get using the grading scale in use in your district/school.

| Name | Lab Reports | | | | | | | | | | Total | Tests/Exams | | | Total | Miscellaneous* | | | | | | Final Total | Final Grade | |
|---|---|---|---|---|---|---|---|---|---|---|---|---|---|---|---|---|---|---|---|---|---|---|---|---|
| out of | 10 | 10 | 10 | 10 | 10 | 10 | 10 | 10 | 10 | 10 | 100 | 50 | 50 | 100 | 200 | 20 | 20 | 20 | 20 | 20 | 100 | 400 | % | Letter |
| Robin | 6 | 6 | 6 | 6 | 5 | 6 | 6 | 7 | 6 | 6 | 60 | 33 | 39 | 81 | 153 | 15 | 15 | 12 | 0 | 10 | 52 | 265 | 66 | C |
| Kay | 2 | 3 | 5 | 5 | 6 | 6 | 7 | 8 | 9 | 10 | 61 | 11 | 29 | 86 | 126 | 15 | 13 | 18 | 10 | 10 | 66 | 253 | 63 | C |
| Marg | 10 | 10 | A | 10 | 10 | 10 | A | 10 | A | A | 60 | 50 | A | 100 | 150 | 0 | 0 | 0 | 0 | 15 | 15 | 225 | 56 | D |
| Dennis | 9 | 8 | 9 | 8 | 9 | 10 | 9 | 10 | 8 | 9 | 89 | 24 | 24 | 49 | 97 | 20 | 17 | 17 | 20 | 20 | 94 | 280 | 70 | B |
| Peter | 10 | 10 | 9 | 9 | 8 | 8 | 7 | 7 | 6 | 5 | 79 | 45 | 36 | 32 | 113 | 20 | 10 | 15 | 10 | 5 | 60 | 252 | 63 | C |
| Lorna | 10 | 10 | 10 | 10 | 10 | 10 | 10 | 10 | 10 | 10 | 100 | 32 | 29 | 59 | 120 | 20 | 20 | 20 | 20 | 20 | 100 | 320 | 80 | A |
| John | 8 | 8 | 8 | 7 | 9 | 9 | 8 | 9 | 10 | 8 | 84 | 32 | 30 | 57 | 119 | 20 | 8 | 7 | 0 | 5 | 40 | 243 | 61 | C |

A = Absent = 0 (for Lab Reports and Tests/Exams)
**\*Miscellaneous**
1-Attendance; 2-Care of Equipment; 3-Attitude/Participation; 4-Notebook; 5-Reading Reports (4x5 marks)
**Letter Grade Legend (in Ontario)**
A = 80%–100%; B = 70%–79%; C = 60%–69%; D = 50%–59%; F = 0%–49%
*Note: This chart was adapted with permission from workshop material presented by Todd Rogers, University of Alberta.*

One A, one B, four Cs, and a D in Ontario—but, did they go to the right students? Marg got the D, but on her achievement alone she probably earned the A. Lorna got the A, but had only a 60% average on tests and exams; is she a weak student who is a teacher's pet—one who receives good marks on the things she can get help on—or is she a very capable student who suffers from severe test anxiety? Kay and Peter both get the same grade but Kay is getting high 80s at the end, whereas Peter is receiving failing marks; is this fair? These are just some of the considerations that arise from an analysis of this case study.

## Case Study 3: Hiring a Student

Very often, secondary report cards give little more information than the student's grade and a three or four word comment. Case Study 3 provides an opportunity to analyze how grades are calculated and whether grades provide meaningful information to potential employers, the students themselves, and their parents.

**Case Study 3: Reflection**

1. To which student would you give a job at the local gas station, based on the information from Scenario 1?

2. Study the additional information in Scenario 2. Which student would get the job now?

3. What grading issues arise from this case study?

Scenario 1
**AUTO MECHANICS**

| Student #1 | | | Student #2 |
|---|---|---|---|
| 71% | | | 52% |

Scenario 2
**WEIGHTS**

| Scenario | Practical | Theory | Grade |
|---|---|---|---|
| A (same as scenario) | 25% | 75% | |
| Student 1 | 0/25 | 71/75 | 71% |
| Student 2 | 25/25 | 27/75 | 52% |
| B | 50% | 50% | |
| Student 1 | 0/50 | 47/50 | 47% |
| Student 2 | 50/50 | 18/50 | 68% |
| C | 75% | 25% | |
| Student 1 | 0/75 | 24/25 | 24% |
| Student 2 | 25/75 | 9/25 | 84% |

This may appear to be an extreme example, but there have been—and probably still are—many classrooms where this situation exists. This case study illustrates the critical connection between teacher's intent and how grades are actually calculated.

## Case Study 4: Anita's Grade?

Number crunching again. Case Study 4 provides many numbers and therefore many possibilities for how grades are calculated.

The teacher of this class bases grades only on unit tests, but believes in multiple assessment opportunities, when it is feasible. Thus on test 2, there are questions on unit 1 and unit 2, on test 3 there are questions on units 1, 2, and 3, and on test 4, there are questions on all four units. This gives students four opportunities to demonstrate their knowledge and skill on unit 1, three opportunities on unit 2, two opportunities on unit 3, but only one opportunity on unit 4. This approach yields many numbers for Anita, as shown in this chart.

**Case Study 4: Reflection**

1. Which grade would you give to Anita? Would you use alternative A, B, C or something else? Why?

2. What grading issues arise from this case study?

| | | TESTS | | |
|---|---|---|---|---|
| Unit | | Score (percentage) | | |
| 1 | 50/100 (50) | 30/50 (60) | 30/40 (75) | 23/25 (92) |
| 2 | | 30/50 (60) | 23/33 (70) | 21/25 (84) |
| 3 | | | 20/30 (67) | 19/25 (76) |
| 4 | | | | 17/25 (72) |
| Test Average | 50% | 60% | 71% | 81% |

Using traditional approaches, there are at least three alternatives for calculating the final grade for Anita:

Alternative A: use the average mark on each test, that is, $(50 + 60 + 71 + 81)/4 = 66\%$

Alternative B: use the final mark on each unit, that is, the marks for each unit on test 4, that is, $(92 + 84 + 76 + 72)/4 = 81\%$

Alternative C: use the mark for the first test on each unit, that is, $(50 + 60 + 67 + 72)/4 = 63\%$

As you can see, these three approaches result in a final grade for Anita that ranges from 63% to 81%, a variation of almost 20%.

One would hope that the teacher would use alternative B because it is the option that provides multiple opportunities and supports the teacher's intent. However, there are many teachers who would use alternative A, and some who would use alternative C, even though it completely negates the multiple assessment opportunities.

## Case Study 5: Grading Scales

What does A mean? What does F mean? For 40 and more years, the author, as a student and as a teacher, in Australia and in Canada, has known that an A has been 80% and an F has been less than 50%. Anything different is very hard for me to comprehend. The familiar becomes the norm—but is it right? Case Study 5 shows readers that letter grades, honors, and pass/fail mean very different things in different educational jurisdictions.

**Case Study 5: Reflection**

1. How do you react to the wide variation in grading scales?

2. What letter grade would Anita (Case Study 4) get if she were in each of these school jurisdictions?

3. What grading issues arise from this case study?

**GRADING SCALES**

Symbol Conversion

| Source | A | B | C | D | F |
|---|---|---|---|---|---|
| Ontario | 80–100% | 70–79% | 60–69% | 50–59% | <50% |
| Ruth Evans* | 90–100% | 80–89% | 70–79% | 60–69% | <60% |
| Rick Werkheiser* | 93–100% | 85–92% | 78–84% | 70–77% | <70% |
| Pam Painter* | 95–100% | 85–94% | 75–84% | 65–74% | <65% |
| R. L. Canady** | 95–100% | 88–94% | 81–87% | 75–80% | <75% |
| Your District | | | | | |

*From World Wide Web, *The School House Teachers' Lounge* (Nebraska)
**Reported in R. L. Canady and P. R. Hotchkiss, "It's a Good Score: Just a Bad Grade," *Phi Delta Kappan,* September 1989, 69.

The chart above shows grading scales used in North America at five different places. You may use the last row to enter the grading scale used in your district/school.

---

# Traditional Inventory for Middle School Grading

| Evaluation Category | Expected Range |
|---|---|
| 1. Quizzes/Tests/Exams | 20–30% |
| 2. Written Assignments<br>creative or explanatory paragraphs, essays, notes,<br>organizers, writing folios, or portfolios | 15–25% |
| 3. Oral Presentations or Demonstrations<br>brief or more formal presentations or demonstrations,<br>role-playing, debates, skits, etc. | 15–25% |
| 4. Projects/Assignments<br>research tasks, hands-on projects, video- or audiotape<br>productions, analysis of issues, etc. | 10–20% |
| 5. Cooperative Group Learning<br>evaluation of the process and skills learned as an<br>individual and as a group member | 5–15% |
| 6. Independent Learning<br>individual organizational skills, contributions to<br>class activities and discussions, homework, notebooks | 5–15% |

---

Figure Intro.5

An A can mean anything from 80% to 95%, a failing grade can be any-where between 49% and 74%. What do these variations mean? For example, is a 49% in Ontario the same as 74% in the district identified by Canady and Hotchkiss as having the highest grade equivalents? There is no way of knowing this without comparing marked student work from both jurisdictions, but the wide variation makes one wonder about the meaning of grades.

## Case Study 6: Grading Inventories

Case Study 6 looks at the recipes teachers use to "cook up" their grades. This case study lets teachers examine how their recipe—or inventory—compares with those of their colleagues.

In most traditional grading situations (see Figure Intro.5 above), teachers have a recipe or inventory for the ingredients in their grades. These usually include some assessment methods and some student behaviors. In addition to the components of grades, such inventories usually include some indication of the relative importance of each component by giving it a (percentage) weight.

**Case Study 6: Reflection**

Use the following chart, Grading Inventory, to identify the grading "recipe" you use. Ask several colleagues in your school to share their inventories. If the categories do not match yours, enter your categories at the bottom.

1. What similarities—or differences—are there between your inventory and those of your colleagues?

2. Why do these differences exist? Should these differences exist?

3. What grading issues arise from this case study?

## Grading Inventory

| Items Included in Grades | Percentages Allocated | | | |
|---|---|---|---|---|
| | Self | Teacher #1 | Teacher #2 | Teacher #3 |
| Exams | | | | |
| Tests | | | | |
| Projects<br>- individual<br>- group | | | | |
| Demonstrations/Oral Presentations | | | | |
| Written Assignments<br>- small writing tasks<br>- writing folders or portfolios<br>- essays | | | | |
| Class Participation and Effort<br>- whole class discussions<br>- group discussions<br>- homework<br>- notebook<br>- attendance, punctuality | | | | |
| Peer Evaluation | | | | |
| Self-Evaluation | | | | |
| (Additional Categories) | | | | |

There is clearly no right answer or perfect grading inventory, but for those who teach the same grade or course(s) in the same school and, ideally, in the same school district, it would not be unreasonable to expect that there would be some basic similarities or discernible patterns in their grading inventories. If there is not, there is need for serious professional discussion about how grading is carried out.

### Case Study 7: Grading Practices That Inhibit Learning

Canady and Hotchkiss (1989) identified 12 grading practices that inhibit learning, which are shown in Figure Intro.6. Many of these are quite common practices that many—or maybe even most—teachers would consider acceptable and normal. The fact that Canady and Hotchkiss labeled them as practices that inhibit learning requires teachers to carefully analyze their own grading practices.

**Case Study 7: Reflection**

1. Which, if any, of the practices identified by Canady and Hotchkiss in Figure Intro.6 as inhibiting learning do you use?

2. What grading issues arise from this case study?

# Grading Practices That Inhibit Learning

1. **Inconsistent grading scales**

   The same performance results in different grades, in different schools or classes.

2. **Worshipping averages**

   Insisting on using all of the math to calculate an average, even when "the average" is not consistent with what the teacher knows about the student's learning.

3. **Using zeros indiscriminately**

   Giving zeros for incomplete work has a devasting effect on averages and often zeros are not even related to learning or achievement but to nonacademic factors like behavior, respect, punctuality, etc.

4. **Following the pattern of assign, test, grade, and teach**

   When teaching occurs after a grade has been assigned, it is too late for the students. They need lots of teaching and practice that is not graded, although it should be assessed and used to enhance learning before testing takes place.

5. **Failing to match testing to teaching**

   Too many teachers rely on trick questions, new formats, and unfamiliar material. If students are expected to perform skills and produce information for a grade, these should be part of the instruction.

6. **Ambushing students**

   Pop quizzes are more likely to teach students how to cheat on a test than to result in learning. Such tests are often control vehicles designed to get even, not to aid understanding.

7. **Suggesting that success is unlikely**

   Students are not likely to strive for targets that they already know are unattainable to them.

8. **Practising "gotcha" teaching**

   A nearly foolproof way to inhibit student learning is to keep the outcomes and expectations of their classes secret. Tests become ways of finding out how well students have read their teacher's mind.

9. **Grading first efforts**

   Learning is not a "one-shot" deal. When the products of learning are complex and sophisticated, students need lots of teaching, practice, and feedback before the product is evaluated.

10. **Penalizing students for taking risks**

    Taking risks is not often rewarded in school. Students need encouragement and support, not low marks, while they try new or more demanding work.

11. **Failing to recognize measurement error**

    Very often grades are reported as objective statistics without attention to weighting factors or the reliability of the scores. In most cases, a composite score may be only a rough estimate of student learning, and sometimes it can be very inaccurate.

12. **Establishing inconsistent grading criteria**

    Criteria for grading in schools and classes often change from day to day, grading period to grading period, and class to class. This lack of consensus makes it difficult for students to understand the rules.

Adapted with permission from R. L. Canady and P. R. Hotchkiss, "It's a Good Score: Just a Bad Grade." *Phi Delta Kappan* (September, 1989): 68–71.

Figure Intro.6

Numbers 2, 3, 4, and 9 in Figure Intro.6 were all part of the author's practices when he was a classroom teacher just a few years ago. Most teachers will probably admit that they use at least one-third of the practices listed at least some of the time. The grading guidelines presented in this book, when fully implemented, eliminate most of these learning inhibiting practices.

## Grading Issues

The case studies have led to the identification of many issues. These grading issues are summarized in this list:

> Ingredients—achievement, ability, effort, attitude/behavior

> Sources of information—paper-and-pencil tests, instructional questions, homework assignments, performance assessments, intuitions, feelings

> Standards—grade distribution

> Weighting and record keeping

> How much data? How recent?

> Student understanding

Although this list is highly generalized, I think it includes all the major grading issues.

### Reflecting on . . . Grading Issues

1. How does this list of grading issues compare with your list? Which issues that you identified are included?

2. Which issues that you identified are not included?

Now that we have identified these issues, let us look at each more closely.

### Ingredients

Teachers include and mix many ingredients to arrive at grades. Student characteristics often used in the mix are achievement, ability, effort, attitude, behavior, participation, and attendance. These ingredients are included because grades serve so many purposes. The result is that grades frequently become almost meaningless for their main purpose—communication. This is clearly illustrated in "Rick's Mysterious Falling Grade," a case that begins Chapter 1.

**Teachers include and mix many ingredients to arrive at grades.**

In order to provide effective communication, grades must be clearly understood by the message senders (teachers and schools) and by the message receivers (students, parents, college admissions officers, employers, etc.). "To develop this shared understanding, there must be a consistent and limited basis for what is included in grades; instead of including everything, we must limit the variables or valued attributes that are included in grades" (O'Connor 1995, 94).

Frisbie and Waltman (1992, 38) provided a very helpful way of looking at this issue. They identified a large set of *evaluation* variables, which includes everything (or almost everything) students do in the classroom and the school. This large set of evaluation variables is reduced to a smaller subset of *reporting* variables. The size of this subset depends on what type of reporting to parents is done by each school/district. Care should be taken to ensure that the most highly valued variables are included. The last step is to select a subset of the reporting variables as the *grading* variables. The grading variables should be those things that are the "status indicators at the end of the learning experience" (Frisbie and Waltman 1992, 38).

Guskey (1994, 17) provided another approach to identifying the ingredients in grades. He identified *progress* criteria, for improvement scoring or learning gain; *process* criteria, for work habits, attendance, participation, effort, and so forth; and *product* criteria, for final exams, overall assessments, or other culminating demonstrations of learning.

Frisbie and Waltman's and Guskey's concepts are combined as shown in Figure Intro.7. This diagram shows that in Frisbie and Waltman's terms,

**Grades must be clearly understood by the message senders and by the message receivers.**

ASSESSMENT and EVALUATION VARIABLES **include**

REPORTING VARIABLES, (process criteria and progress criteria)

**and** GRADING VARIABLES (product criteria)

**Figure Intro.7** Adapted with permission from K. O'Connor "Guidelines for Grading That Support Learning and Student Success." *NASSP Bulletin*, (April, 1998): 24–28, National Association of Secondary School Principals.

SkyLight Training and Publishing Inc

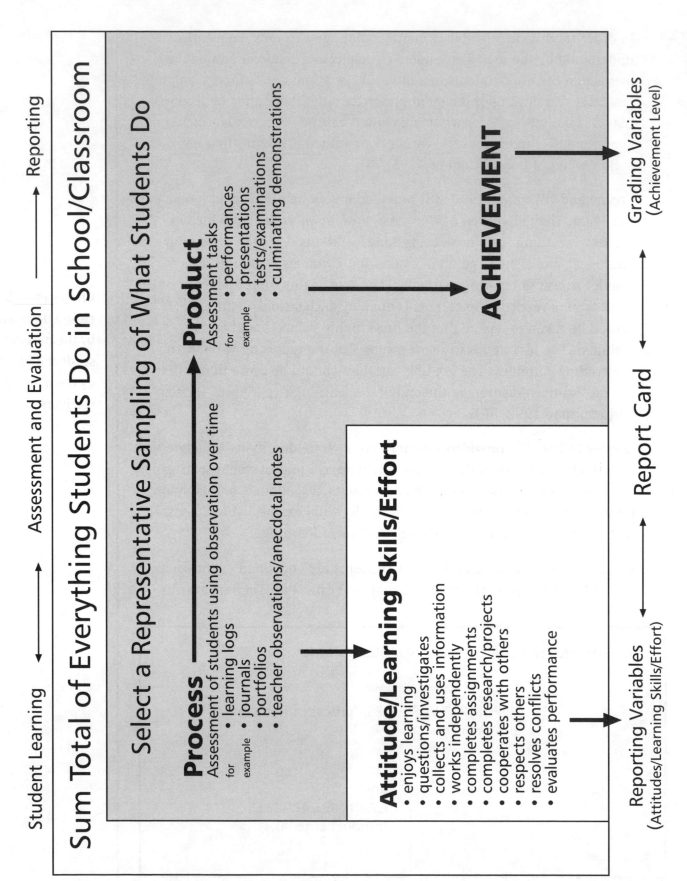

# Sum Total of Everything Students Do in School/Classroom

## Select a Representative Sampling of What Students Do

Student Learning ←→ Assessment and Evaluation ←→ Reporting

### Process
Assessment of students using observation over time

for · learning logs
example · journals
· portfolios
· teacher observations/anecdotal notes

### Product
Assessment tasks

for · performances
example · presentations
· tests/examinations
· culminating demonstrations

**ACHIEVEMENT**

### Attitude/Learning Skills/Effort
· enjoys learning
· questions/investigates
· collects and uses information
· works independently
· completes assignments
· completes research/projects
· cooperates with others
· respects others
· resolves conflicts
· evaluates performance

Grading Variables
(Achievement Level)

←→ Report Card ←→

Reporting Variables
(Attitudes/Learning Skills/Effort)

Adapted from the work of author (Ken O'Connor) and Damian Cooper, Halton District School, Ontario.     Figure Intro.8

SkyLight Training and Publishing Inc

Guskey's process and progress criteria are the reporting (and evaluation) variables, and the product criteria are the grading variables. This combination identifies variables that are separated for grading and reporting purposes. The interaction shown in Figure Intro.7, however, is rather simplistic, as some process variables may be assessed over time as part of stated learning goals, and, therefore, may legitimately be considered as grading variables. This more complex and more realistic identification of grading and reporting variables is illustrated in Figure Intro.8.

## Sources of Information

Teachers have many possible sources of information about student achievement. Teachers use a wide variety of assessment methods, but not all sources of information need be included in grades. Decisions about which sources of information to include are based on the reliability and validity of the data and the purpose of the assessment. Teachers make these decisions consciously and carefully.

## Standards

In order for grades to have any real meaning, they must be related to some type of standard—norm, criterion, or self-referenced. Traditionally, grades have been *norm-referenced*, that is, they were based on comparing the individual with a group. This frequently involved the use of the bell curve or some modification of the curve.

With the introduction of state and local standards, grades are increasingly based on these standards and so are *criterion-referenced*. Even where there are no published standards, teachers use criterion-referenced standards when they provide their students with rubrics—scoring scales that clearly indicate the criteria for quality work.

*Self-referenced* standards, which compare students with their own previous performance, can also provide valuable information.

The issue that needs to be considered is which type of standard to use to determine grades and which type to use only in report card comments.

## Weighting and Record Keeping

Because there are many ingredients in grades, even if only achievement information is used, teachers have to decide the relative importance of

**Grades are increasingly criterion-referenced.**

the various components. This is usually done by setting different percentages or weights for each of the various ingredients. This is a key area for subjectivity—that is, carefully thought out and logically justifiable professional judgment. It is an issue because careful thought and logical justification are frequently forgotten.

Record keeping is also important. The complexity of learning goals requires that teachers base grades on complete and accurate tabulated records—on paper, on a computer, or both. It is not justifiable for data that go into a grade to come off the top of a teacher's head at the end of the grading period.

### How Much Data? How Recent?

Teachers tend to include everything that they score in student grades. The issue to consider is whether all these data are necessary or appropriate. The amount of data needed is only that which enables confidence that any further information will confirm the previous judgment. Focus should be on the highest consistent level of performance toward the end of any learning (grading) period because this is the information that tells whether the learning goals have been met.

### Student Understanding

Frequently students do not understand how the grades they received were determined. This occurs because either the grading procedures were not discussed with them or the procedures are too complicated to be understood. The issue is how teachers may best ensure that students understand their grades. If grades are to serve learning, there must be understanding and involvement.

## Guidelines for Grading

Grading issues can be addressed in a variety of ways. To avoid the misuse and misinterpretation of grades, a set of grading guidelines that address the practical concerns of teachers is needed.

Traditional grading practices need to change so that grading aligns with and supports current assessment and evaluation philosophy and practices.

The grading guidelines in Figure Intro.9 on page 34 were developed with these principles in mind. Some of them require radical changes in teacher practices, especially at the high school and college levels, and in school and district policies. The guidelines are organized in approximate order of

> The complexity of learning goals requires that teachers base grades on complete and accurate tabulated records.

importance to the support of student learning and success and, together, make a consistent group. The order also relates to where most change from traditional grading practices is needed—relatively few teachers using traditional approaches to grading use Guidelines 1, 2, or 3, whereas many (maybe most) teachers already follow Guidelines 7 and 8.

The specific relationships between the grading issues identified and the guidelines are shown in Figure Intro.10 on page 35. Each issue relates primarily to one guideline.

This set of grading guidelines has been modified considerably from those proposed by Gronlund and Linn (1990, 443), but it is important to acknowledge that their list was the starting point. Guidelines such as these are more practical than most guidelines one can find in the literature on grading. They are intended to provide practical guidance to teachers as they decide how to grade students' achievement—and can actually be used by teachers in their grade books or in setting up their computer grading programs. Guidelines also need to have school and/or district policy status, so that students and parents can understand the grading practices used in their classrooms, and so that they can expect grading practices that are consistent among all teachers in each school. Currently, teachers are "all over the book"; these guidelines should at least get teachers in the same chapter and, eventually, on the same page!

In Chapters 1 through 8, each guideline is examined individually in detail.

> **Guidelines are intended to provide practical guidance to teachers as they grade students' achievement.**

## Reflecting on . . . the Guidelines

1. What is your initial reaction to each of the guidelines for grading on page 34? Why?

2. Think in terms of what is **P**ositive, what is a **C**oncern, and what is just **I**nteresting (PCI). List your reflections for later reference.

# Guidelines for Grading

## To Support Learning, To Encourage Student Success

1. Individual achievement is the only basis for grades.

2. Sample student performance—do not mark everything and do not include all marks in grades.

3. Grade in pencil—keep records so they may be updated easily.

4. Relate grading procedures to learning goals (expectations, standards, etc.).

5. Crunch numbers carefully.

6. Use criterion-referenced (i.e., absolute or preset) standards to distribute grades and marks.

7. Use quality assessments and properly record evidence of achievement.

8. Discuss assessment, including grading, with students at the beginning of instruction.

# The Relationship Between Grading Issues and the Grading Guidelines

| Grading Issue | Guideline |
|---|---|
| Ingredients | 1 |
| Sources of information | 2, 4 |
| Standards (grade distribution) | 6 |
| Weighting | 5 |
| Record keeping | 7 |
| How much data? | 2 |
| How recent? | 3 |
| Student understanding | 8 |

Figure Intro.10

# CHAPTER 1

# GRADING INDIVIDUAL ACHIEVEMENT

*Grades should not be used to control student behavior . . . . It is tempting to use them to maintain discipline. However, the grades then lose their meaning as indicators of achievement. It is better to show students that how they act affects the way they learn and to use learning as the basis for their rewards.*

—Schafer (1997, 545)

| GUIDELINE | **Individual achievement is the only basis for grades.** |
| --- | --- |
| **1** | |

## The Case of Rick's Mysterious Falling Grade

The report card mathematics grade that Rick received in December in Grade 8 was about 25% lower than the grade he received in June at the end of Grade 7. His parents were very concerned because Rick had always enjoyed mathematics and achieved at a high level. They went to the parent-teacher conference wondering whether he needed a tutor. When they put this question to his teacher, she said that this was not necessary. She went on to say that his mathematics results were excellent; all his test scores were more than 80%, but that he had received low marks for participation, effort, group work, notebook, homework, and so forth. Rick's parents felt the grade was very misleading because it did not indicate clearly Rick's level of mathematics achievement.

## What's the Purpose of the Guideline?

This guideline is number one because, among the many purposes for grades, the first is communication—with students, parents, and many others—of the achievement status of each student.

## What Are the Key Elements of the Guideline?

### Grading Achievement Only

For grades to have real meaning, they must be relatively pure measures of each student's achievement of the learning goals for each course. Achievement may be defined narrowly as knowledge, somewhat more broadly as knowledge and skills, or most broadly as knowledge, skills, and behavior. The breadth of definition of achievement depends on the stated, clearly understood learning goals. For example, in a senior mathematics or science course, achievement may be defined quite narrowly, whereas in a freshman drama, environmental studies, or physical education course, achievement could, and probably should, be defined more broadly. The

**For grades to have real meaning, they must be relatively pure measures of each student's achievement of the learning goals.**

breadth of definition of achievement varies with the grade level and the nature of the course.

## Grading Viewpoints

A number of viewpoints relevant to this guideline can be found in the literature on grading. A selection of viewpoints follows.

Stiggins and Knight described the situation portrayed in "Rick's Mysterious Falling Grade" as grade pollution (1997, 60). They said that "when the object is effective communication [of achievement] . . . schools [should] adopt grading policies that permit teachers to indicate each student's current level of academic achievement with nothing else factored in to interfere with that message" (61).

Brookhart stated that teachers' grading practices often combine a variety of factors "into composite scores of questionable validity and uncertain meaning" (1994, 299).

Bailey and McTighe noted that "grades often reflect a combination of achievement, progress, and other factors. . . . this tendency to collapse several independent elements into a single grade may blur their meaning" (1996, 121).

Cizek found that teachers created what he calls "an uncertain mix." By an uncertain mix, he means that they "combined the marks they had assigned to individual assignments and tests, . . . with three other kinds of information:

- formal achievement-related measures (attendance, class participation);

- informal achievement-related measures (answers in class, one-on-one discussions); and

- other informal information (impressions of effort, conduct, teamwork, leadership and so on)." (1996a, December, 104–105)

He concludes that "this mix of factors is difficult to disentangle."

Hensley reported that "class attendance and 'dressing out' were the most frequently used variables in the assessment of students in physical education classes" (1989, 38). This finding was supported by Matanin and Tannehill who stated that "factors that stood out as consistent contributors to students' grades in physical education were attendance, appropriate attire, behavior and effort" (1994, 403). Canady, in a workshop in

**Grades often reflect a combination of achievement, progress, and other factors . . . this tendency to collapse several independent elements into a single grade may blur their meaning. (Bailey and McTighe 1996, 121)**

Toronto in June 1996 described this as determining grades on whether their shorts were clean and whether their socks matched!

Gronlund and Linn stated that

> letter grades are likely to be most meaningful and useful when they represent achievement only. If they are contaminated by such extraneous factors as effort, the amount of work completed (rather than the quality of the work), personal conduct and so on, their interpretation will be hopelessly confused. When letter grades combine various aspects of pupil development, not only do they lose their meaning as a measure of achievement, but they also suppress information concerning other important aspects of development. (1990, 437)

## A Critical Grading Concept: Achievement

The basic concepts embodied in this guideline are illustrated in Figure Intro.8. This diagram shows that teachers make some sort of assessment of everything that students do in the school or classroom (the outer rectangle), but from that entirety, they select a representative sampling of what students do to grade and/or to report. The grading variables concentrate on achievement of the process and product learning goals, whereas attitude, learning skills, and effort are seen primarily as reporting variables. *Achievement* demonstrates knowledge, skills, and behaviors that are stated as learning objectives for a course or unit of instruction.

This guideline does not imply that grading is simply a clinical, objective procedure. There is a great deal of professional judgment involved in grading, as teachers develop an assessment plan (Guideline 8), choose or develop the assessment instruments (Guideline 7), evaluate the process and product components of grades (Guidelines 2 and 3), and record the results after deciding how to combine the scores and calculate grades (Guidelines 4, 5, and 6). These aspects are considered in later discussions of the guidelines.

A critical aspect of Guideline 1 is this: Grades are limited to individual achievement and are not used as punishment for poor attendance, inappropriate behavior, or lack of punctuality. These are discipline problems and, although they usually impact on achievement, they should be dealt with as such. Most schools have rules or student codes of behavior that set standards and penalties; penalties for rule or code infractions should not be academic penalties. Lowering grades simply because of poor attendance, misbehavior, or lateness distorts achievement; grades then do not have clear meaning. Bobby's C may reflect his consistent achievement

**A critical aspect of Guideline 1 is this: Grades are limited to individual achievement and are not used as punishment.**

at that level, whereas Ann's C, although she consistently achieves at an A level, results from her many absences, frequent lateness, and misbehavior. This mixed result is inconsistent with this guideline; schools or districts that have such penalties in their grading policies need to move them to their discipline policies and also ensure that their formal and informal communication vehicles allow them to report poor behavior, attendance, and lateness in an accurate and timely manner. Hills provides an excellent analysis of how to deal with attendance.

> If the desired behavior or competency is to attend class regularly, then have that as a written objective and base grades on it. (For most courses above the primary grades, this approach would be absurd.) If the desired behavior or competency is a skill in the topic under study, such as effective behavior in an operating room, then base the grade solely on the level of skill achieved in that behavior. If a student is able to develop that skill without attending, then his or her atten-dance is irrelevant as far as an evaluation of competence is con-cerned. If some students are truant, and if this situation influences the behavior of other students, then you have a disciplinary problem, and you should deal with it as a disciplinary matter, not as an aca-demic matter. If the student cannot be evaluated on something like skill and effectiveness in the operating room because no one has seen him or her function in one, then no grade should be given at all. You have no basis for determining a level of competency, so you should not pretend otherwise. (1991, 541)

A particularly difficult aspect of misbehavior is the issue of cheating, because it crosses the line between behavior and achievement. Schools and districts need procedures to deal fairly and appropriately with cheat-ing, including plagiarism. As with other misbehavior, cheating is primarily a discipline problem, but it clearly is reasonable to have more direct academic consequences for this than for other behavioral problems. An excellent case study that illustrates this issue can be found in Busick and Stiggins (1997, 109–110).

## Grading Individuals

Another extremely important aspect of this guideline is the emphasis on grading individuals on their personal achievement rather than grading individuals on their group's achievement. With the increasing importance of the ability to work effectively with others in school and at work, this emphasis on individual achievement may seem strange. But remember that students' grades appear on their personal report cards and therefore

**Schools or districts that have absence, lateness, and misbe-havior penalties in their grading policies need to move them to their discipline policies.**

should not be contaminated by the achievement (or lack of achievement) of other students.

### Concerns About Group Grades

It is unfortunate that group marks are one of the reasons why students and parents give group work a bad name. Cooperative learning, despite its importance for the development of capable citizens and productive employees and its value to learning as shown by a significant body of research, has had to struggle against this legacy.

In his excellent article, Kagan (1995) provided strong criticism of eight arguments for group grades (see Figure 1.1), gave seven reasons why he is "unequivocally opposed to group grades" (69; see Figure 1.2), and then suggested "alternative ways to accomplish the same goals" (71). (Please note that in most cases, Kagan uses *grade* to mean what this book calls *mark*.) Kagan also suggested that cooperative learning skills can be rewarded through a variety of other recognition approaches that are more effective than group grades (71). He said that it is preferable to give students a mark in "group skills" or marks in specific cooperative skills.

Rather than use group marks, Kagan (1995) proposed several alternatives:

1. Follow an approach similar to Kohn's 3 Cs (1993a, 212–221) so that "we will not need grades to motivate students. (71)" [Kohn's 3 Cs are collaboration—learning together, content—things worth knowing, and choice—autonomy in the classroom.]

2. Provide formal feedback in written form on students' cooperative learning skills. Kagan believes students will work very hard if they know in advance that such feedback will occur.

3. "Meet with students individually after asking them to set their own goals" (71). This type of self-assessment promotes real learning.

### Marking Cooperative Learning

How then should cooperative learning be marked? Obviously, the key is to focus on assessing the skills of each student as an individual. One way to do this is to use an observation sheet such as shown in Figure 1.3.

While students are working on a cooperative learning task, the teacher walks around the classroom and records information on each group. Observations may be made by the teacher, by students of other students, or by students of themselves, but are restricted to two or three skills at

> Students' grades appear on their personal report cards and therefore should not be contaminated by the achievement (or lack of achievement) of other students.

# Kagan's Critique of Group Grades

| Argument | Counter Argument |
|---|---|
| **The real-world argument**—preparing students for the real world requires that they develop cooperative learning skills; in the real world, teams are rewarded for their group effort. | **BUT** "in the real world there are many unfair practices, . . . that doesn't justify unfair practices in the classroom." (68) |
| **The employment-skills argument**—grading the social skill of cooperation, which is highly desired by employers, shows students that it is important. | **BUT** "group grades don't necessarily foster social skills," (68) and "group grades on academic projects do not fairly assess the cooperative skills of individuals because, for example, if most members of the group cooperate very well, everyone in the group—even the least cooperative student—receives a high grade. The reverse is also true and is probably a more serious problem." |
| **The motivation argument**—students won't work together unless it counts in the grade. | **BUT** "there are many better ways to motivate students." (69) |
| **The teachers' workload argument**—some teachers prefer marking groups because it is faster than marking many individual papers. | **BUT** "this is not a legitimate short cut. Group grades tell us nothing reliable about individual performance." (69) |
| **The grades-are-subjective-anyway argument.** | **BUT** "the sometimes subjective nature of grading does not justify using a method that is even less precise." (69) |
| **The grades-aren't-that-important argument.** | **BUT** "try explaining it to the parents of a student who, based on his or her grades [which included group marks for cooperation], has just narrowly missed being accepted to a desired college." (69) |
| **The credit-for-teamwork argument.** | **BUT** "individuals should be given credit for their individual work, not a free ride on the work of others." (69) |
| **The group-grades-are-a-small-factor argument**—some argue that it is all right to use group marks because they rarely have a significant impact on the final grade. | **BUT** "very occasionally is far too often if it means giving individual grades which do not reflect individual performances." (69) |

Adapted with permission from S. Kagan, "Group Grades Miss the Mark," *Educational Leadership* (May, 1995): 68–71.

Figure 1.1

SkyLight Training and Publishing Inc

# Kagan's Seven Reasons
# for Opposing Group Grades

**1** **"No fair."** "Group grades are so blatantly unfair that on this basis alone they should never be used." (69)

**2** **"Group grades debase report cards."** (70) The issue here is that, if the grade a student gets "is a function of who the student happens to have as a teammate," then no one can use the grades in a meaningful way.

**3** **"Group grades undermine motivation."** (70) There are two problems here: (1) group grades penalize students who work hard but have cooperative learning partners who don't, and (2) they reward students who don't work hard but have hard-working partners. Both scenarios have undesirable effects on student motivation.

**4** **"Group grades convey the wrong message."** (70) Grading practices send students messages about what is valued. The basic point of the guidelines presented in this book is that grading should emphasize and support learning and success, but if grades "are partially a function of forces entirely out of their control" (70), it sends entirely the wrong message to students.

**5** **"Group grades violate individual accountability."** (70) This is a key principle of cooperative learning. If it is applied effectively and appropriately, students are likely to achieve more; if not, students will find ways to manipulate the situation to their personal advantage.

**6** **"Group grades are responsible for parents', teachers', and students' resistance to cooperative learning."** (70)

**7** **"Group grades may be challenged in court."** (71)

Adapted with permission from S. Kagan, "Group Grades Miss the Mark," *Educational Leadership* (May, 1995): 68–71.

Figure 1.2

SkyLight Training and Publishing Inc

# Group Cooperative Learning Assessment

Assessor:    Teacher ☐    Peer ☐    Self ☐

Put the appropriate symbol in the boxes for each student.

Evidence of skill observed ✓    Not observed yet ✗

| Cooperative learning skill \ Names of students in the group | Student 1 | Student 2 | | | | | | |
|---|---|---|---|---|---|---|---|---|
| Stays focused on task | | | | | | | | |
| Fulfills assigned role | | | | | | | | |
| Contributes ideas and solutions | | | | | | | | |
| Works well with others (listens, shares, and supports others) | | | | | | | | |
| Shows interest and involvement | | | | | | | | |
| *Additional skills (developed by teachers and students)* | | | | | | | | |

Reprinted with permission, ©1995 Toronto District School Board, Ontario, Canada.

Figure 1.3

any one time. Feedback is given to individuals, to groups, and to the class as a whole. After students practice their cooperative skills and observation skills, then a sheet, patterned on Figure 1.3, can be used to summarize each student's achievement in this area. If necessary, this summary can be converted to marks (see Chapter 5) for inclusion in student grades.

A variety of approaches to assessing cooperative learning were suggested by Sheeran (1994). He emphasized individual accountability and positive interdependence. However, a number of the methods he suggested are of dubious merit because they are based on the concept of individuals receiving bonus marks when group goals are achieved, for example, an average score on a test. This is inappropriate for two reasons: (1) an individual's mark depends on the efforts of others, and (2) bonus marks are not acceptable in any circumstances. Although positive, bonus marks distort achievement grades because they mix other factors with achievement. It is better not to use them—if students do something worthy of extra credit, consider it to be a reporting variable and recognize the exceptional achievement with either a formal (report card) or informal (note or phone call) communication.

**Bonus marks distort achievement grades because they mix other factors with achievement. It is better not to use them.**

Another approach to marking group projects was suggested by Culp and Malone. For them, student contributions to such projects "fall into four main categories: creativity/ideas contributed, research/data collection, writing/typing/artwork, and organizing/collating" (1992, 35). Students rate each other's contributions in each category with the total for each category for all students adding up to one hundred percent. Comparisons are made between student and teacher ratings to ensure that they are fair. The average for each student is then converted to a percentage mark. Culp and Malone suggested that keeping scores over several projects provides useful information—students learn more about themselves. They see that individuals contribute differently to the team, and they may identify specific skills they might want to strengthen (1992, 36, 39).

One very significant positive aspect of Culp and Malone's approach is that it overcomes a problem that is seen frequently in the marking of cooperative learning, that is, the rationing of success. They overcome the problem by giving a mark of 95% to each student (in a group of four) whose average contribution is 21% or greater. However, if a percentage contribution of 21% or higher is considered to be exemplary performance, the mark should be 100% for two reasons: students are not arbitrarily penalized, and the maximum score should always be attainable. To paraphrase

Stiggins, any student who hits the goal should get the highest possible mark.

In conclusion, note that "a carefully constructed cooperative environment that offers challenging learning tasks, that allows students to make key decisions about how they perform, and that emphasizes the value (and skills) of helping each other to learn" (Kohn 1991, 86) is far more important than coming up with the perfect way to mark. The various aspects of cooperative learning, as shown in Figure 1.3, can then be included in grades. This is a difficult aspect of marking and grading. The principle to keep in mind is to emphasize individual achievement within the cooperative learning setting.

## What Should Not Be in Grades?

Effort, participation, attitude, and other personal and social characteristics need to be reported separately from achievement. Figure 1.4 shows a grading inventory for a performance subject.

### Reflecting on . . . Grading Inventories

Consider the effects of the grading inventory shown in Figure 1.4 on the following scenarios, in which a block schedule with 70 classes can be assumed:

Scenario 1—a student who missed 10% of the classes would be able to receive a grade of no more than 80%, even if he or she got perfect marks in all other aspects of the course.

Scenario 2—a student who missed 7% of the classes and who was late for 10% of the classes would be able to receive a maximum grade of 82%.

Are these fair results? Does this inventory produce grades with clear meaning? Does a procedure like this promote attendance and punctuality?

Does a procedure like this honor learning?

### Effort

Hard work (effort), frequent responses to teacher questions, intense involvement in class activities (participation), and a positive, encouraging, friendly, and happy demeanor (attitude) are all highly valued attributes, but they should not be included directly in grades because they are very difficult to define and even more difficult to measure.

**Any student who hits the goal should get the highest possible mark.**

# *What Should NOT Be Included in Grades

Extract from an actual high school grading inventory for a performance subject

|  | % of grade |
|---|---|
| *Daily activities | 40% |
| Major projects and performances | 30% |
| Journals (reflections on projects and performances) | 10% |
| *Attendance and Punctuality | 20% |

| **Attendance Scale** | **Late (Tardiness) Scale** |
|---|---|
| 20 marks—perfect attendance | Subtract 1/2 mark—first late |
| 16 marks—3 absences | Subtract 1/2 mark—second late |
| 12 marks—4 absences | Subtract 1 mark—lates |
| 8 marks—5 absences | thereafter |
| 4 marks—6 absences | |
| 0 marks—7 absences | |

Figure 1.4

Stiggins provided a detailed analysis of the arguments for and against including these factors in grades (1997, 417–422). With regard to effort, he said that definitions of trying hard vary greatly from teacher to teacher, and so, if effort is included in the grade, "we add noise into the grade interpretation process" (418). *Noise* means "static; not clear meaningful signals" (413). He also noted that "students can manipulate their apparent level of effort to mislead us" (418).

## Participation

Stiggins suggested that participation is often a personality issue—some students are naturally more assertive while others are naturally quieter. This is often related to gender and/or ethnicity, and so we run the risk of these biases if we include effort and participation in grades. Another problem is that "factoring effort into the grade may send the wrong message to students. In real life just trying hard to do a good job is virtually never enough. If we don't deliver relevant, practical results we will not be deemed successful, regardless of how hard we try" (Stiggins 1997, 418).

The inclusion of attitude presents similar problems; positive attitude has many dimensions, is very difficult to define, and is extremely difficult to

**Factoring effort into the grade may send the wrong message to students. In real life just trying hard to do a good job is virtually never enough.** (Stiggins 1997, 418)

measure. It is also very easy to manipulate—students can fake a positive attitude if they think or know it will help their grade.

To a considerable extent, personal and social characteristics do contribute to achievement, but including a mark for attitude as part of a mark for a product would blur the assessment of the product and affect the validity and thus the meaning of the grade. Also, including a mark for effort or any of these characteristics means a double benefit for successful students and double (or triple or quadruple) jeopardy for less successful students. This is clearly unfair.

Strong effort, active participation, and positive attitude are highly valued attributes, but, if grades are to have clear meaning, they should not be included in grades; they are reporting variables, not grading variables. These attributes need to be assessed as accurately and rigorously as possible and reported separately and regularly. Examples of reporting procedures that include these student characteristics can be found in Chapter 10 in Figure 10.2b.

## Late Work

A major problem that overlaps both parts of this guideline is the issue of submitting required work on time. The following late homework policy for one college course was found on the World Wide Web:

> Homework turned in for grading in class on the date due will incur no penalty. Otherwise the following grade reductions are in effect:
> - up to one day—a 5 percent reduction;
> - two days late—a 10 percent reduction;
> - three days late—a 20 percent reduction;
> - four days late—a 40 percent reduction; and
> - five days late—an 80 percent reduction.
>
> Homework extensions are only granted BEFORE homework is due. Do not attempt to obtain an extension on or after the due date. [Source withheld deliberately]

At the high school level in the author's school district, penalties for handing work in late have been as high as 10% per day to a maximum of 50% (including weekend days!).

There are two problems with these approaches. First, the penalty that students receive distorts their achievement and thus contributes to a mark and, ultimately, to a grade that does not have clear meaning. Second, the

**Strong effort, active participation, and positive attitude are highly valued, but they are reporting, not grading, variables.**

punitive nature of the penalty provides a powerful disincentive for students to complete any work after it is more than one or two days late. In both examples, no intelligent student would bother completing the work after three days. Such policies are obviously opposed to a learning/ success orientation, which holds that it is more important that the work be done and learning occur than when the work is done and the learning occurs. This does not mean that handing work in on time is not important, but as once was said in a lecture, "It is best to do it right and on time, but it is better to do it right and late than the reverse" (specific source unknown).

In the school or college situation, there are several important considerations about due dates for student work. One is that required work is sometimes part of an instructional sequence and so needs to be submitted before marked work is returned. A second consideration is that teachers need to have a reasonable workload—they cannot be expected to mark huge amounts of work on the last day or two of a grading period.

In both the first and the second situations, the concept of an absolute deadline after which no work will be accepted for inclusion in grades—in that grading period—may be appropriate and/or necessary. This does not mean that students automatically receive zeroes or severe penalties. In the case of work in an instructional sequence, this type of work usually has a formative purpose and so is not included in grades anyway (see Chapter 2); all the teacher needs to do is record that the work was not done or was handed in late. In the case of lack of time for the teacher to grade, the most appropriate approach would be to record an incomplete and include the mark in the student's grade in the next grading period, when the teacher has had a reasonable amount of time to assess the student's work.

A third consideration for due dates is that these are frequently quite arbitrary, especially for major performance assessments such as term papers. In these—and in fact, in all—situations, encourage students to submit work on time, but if they do not, keep penalties as small as possible, for example, 1% or 2% per day to a maximum of 10%; record the fact of the tardiness; and consider the fact as a reporting, not a (major) grading, variable.

Think of your favorite author—let us called her Margaret. Imagine that, when Margaret was in high school, she was a brilliant writer but always handed work in late. Using the punitive procedures described above,

> **It is best to do work right and on time, but it is better to do it right and late than the reverse.**

although receiving As or 90% or more on each piece of writing, Margaret would probably have received relatively low grades because her marks would have been reduced one or two letter grades, or 20% to 30%. The final grade would give no idea of her high quality of work or of her tardiness problem. Far better that Margaret get the 90% or better that she deserved as marks and that the report card state—"95%, Margaret is a brilliant writer but she always hands her work in late." Now we have real information. If she is going to be a novelist or a playwright, it is not much of a problem—publishers have deadlines, but for novels and plays, the deadlines are often quite flexible. If, however, she has applied to be a journalist on a daily newspaper or an advertising copywriter, she will probably not be hired because often the time deadlines are more important than the quality of the writing.

It must be emphasized again that the intent here is not to encourage students to hand work in late; the intent is that tardiness be dealt with appropriately, so grades have meaning and communicate clear, easily interpretable information about achievement.

**The intent here is not to encourage students to hand work in late; the intent is that tardiness be dealt with appropriately.**

# What's the Bottom Line?

What should be in grades?—achievement only, defined as broadly or narrowly as professional judgment dictates.

What should not be in grades?—effort, attitude, behavior, attendance, punctuality, tardiness, and so forth.

# What's My Thinking Now?

Analyze Guideline 1 for grading (Individual achievement is the only basis for grades) by focusing on the following three questions:

Why use it?

Why not use it?

Points of uncertainty

After careful thought about these points, answer these two questions:

Would I use Guideline 1 now?

Do I agree or disagree with the guideline, or am I unsure at this time?

(See the following for one person's reflections on Guideline 1.)

# A Reflection on Guideline 1

## WHY USE IT?

- very clear, concrete, and specific
- clarifies priorities
- gives "pure" grades
- gives a clear picture of student achievement, whereas mixing achievement and effort gives a muddy picture of both
- more accountable for really knowing student strengths and weaknesses

## WHY NOT USE IT?

- attitude and effort important in students' future
- lack of clear definition of achievement
- participation and achievement so closely linked
- report card does not allow separation of achievement and effort
- school and district policy

## POINTS OF UNCERTAINTY

- where do participation and effort fit?
- how to include growth?
- employability skills are critical; how to include?
- how to report in a manageable way?
- students need to see consequences of their behavior in an obvious way

## CHAPTER 2

# SAMPLING STUDENT PERFORMANCE

*We know that students will rarely perform at high levels on challenging learning tasks at their first attempt. Deep understanding or high levels of proficiency are achieved only as a result of trial, practice, adjustments based on feedback, and more practice. Performance-based instruction underscores the importance of using assessments to provide information to guide improvement throughout the learning process, instead of waiting to give feedback at the end of instruction.*

—McTighe (1996/1997, 11)

GUIDELINE

2

# Sample student performance —do not mark everything and do not include all marks in grades.

## The Case of Heather's Grim Grade

Heather is a very bright girl who generally achieves at a very high level. She has always liked and done well in English. On her first report card in Grade 11 English, she gets a C; both her parents and Heather are shocked and upset by the low (for her) grade. They express their concern to her teacher, who provides them with a computer printout showing how Heather's C was calculated. What is revealed is that the marks for virtually every piece of work that was done were included in the letter grade. First drafts, experimental pieces, quizzes on spelling and grammar— marks for all of these were included. Heather did not do well on any of these, but her unit tests, final drafts, and a major project all received marks of 85% or better. Heather likes to experiment and to take risks on creative tasks; she also needs a lot of practice to understand concepts and detail. By including all the scores from the formative assessments in her grade, her teacher had emphasized Heather's weaknesses as a learner.

**It is essential that teachers distinguish between *formative* and *summative* assessment.**

## What's the Purpose of the Guideline?

This guideline requires that teachers have a clear understanding of the purpose of each assessment. It is essential that teachers distinguish between *formative* and *summative* assessment. Use formative assessment primarily to give feedback to students (and teachers) on the progress of learning; use summative assessment for judgments, which are included in grades. This approach deals with two serious problems: (1) the does-this-count? syndrome exhibited by students and (2) the I-have-too-much-marking syndrome exhibited by teachers. In high schools, this may be the single most important guideline because many secondary teachers have a strong tendency toward putting a number on everything students do and putting everything into the grade.

# What Are the Key Elements of the Guideline?

## Formative Versus Summative Assessment

It is essential that the concepts of formative and summative assessment be clearly understood. The following definitions are provided in the glossary (Appendix 1):

*Formative.* Assessment designed to provide direction for improvement and/or adjustment to a program for individual students or for a whole class, that is, quizzes, initial drafts/attempts, homework, and questions during instruction.

*Summative.* Assessment/evaluation designed to provide information to be used in making judgments about a student's achievement at the end of a period of instruction, that is, tests, exams, final drafts/attempts, assignments, projects, performances.

Figure 2.1 provides a clear perspective on formative and summative assessment.

## Comparison of Formative and Summative Assessments

| | Formative | Summative |
|---|---|---|
| Purpose | To monitor and guide a process/product while it is still in progress | To judge the success of a process/product at the end (however arbitrarily defined) |
| Time of assessment | During the process or development of the product | At the end of the process or when the product is complete |
| Types of assessment techniques | Informal observation, quizzes, homework, teacher questions, worksheets | Formal observation, tests, projects, term papers, exhibitions |
| Uses of assessment information | To improve and change a process/product while it is still going on/being developed | Judge the quality of a process or product; grade, rank, promote |

Adapted from P. W. Airasian, *Classroom Assessment*, 2nd ed. (New York: McGraw-Hill, 1994), 136.

Figure 2.1

Teachers need a very clear vision of their purpose for each assessment. If assessment is principally to inform learners about their strengths and weaknesses as well as inform teachers about how successful instruction is as it proceeds, then assessment is formative. On the other hand, if assessment is primarily to inform about the achievement status of the learner, then it is summative. Obviously there is some overlap, particularly with summative assessment.

## Assessing Process and Product

It is also extremely important that teachers do not equate process with formative assessment and products with summative assessment. Process may and should be assessed both formatively and summatively; similarly, products may be assessed both formatively and summatively. Furthermore, summative assessments are not only tests and exams; there is a huge variety of assessment methods that can be used summatively. See Figure 2.2.

A good example of a process that can be accessed formatively and summatively is student use of safety skills in a laboratory or vocational program. Starting on the first day, the teacher introduces students to critical safety skills. Students are given or develop clear criteria indicating levels of performance, possibly in the form of a rubric that describes various levels of quality. Students practice their safety skills daily as the teacher observes and feeds back to them information as to their strengths and weaknesses. The teacher keeps track of these observations—these records could be anecdotal, symbols (✔ or x), level scores (1–4), or numbers (e.g., 7/10). This process continues over a number of weeks. Near the end of the first grading period, the teacher announces that, for several specific days, the same criteria and the same observations will be used to assess students' safety skills and that the scores are to be included in their grades. This period of observation becomes the summative assessment of their process skills. No score from the practice weeks is included in the grade. These scores are used instead to provide valuable reporting information about growth and progress.

An example of a performance that can be assessed formatively and summatively is a student seminar presentation (individual or group). Usually, these major projects are scheduled far in advance, so students need some guidance to keep them on track. The teacher may provide students with a schedule for checking such things as hypothesis, first draft, audiovisual needs, and a second draft. Students might also have a

**It is extremely important that teachers do not equate process with formative assessment and products with summative assessment.**

# A Performance May Be...

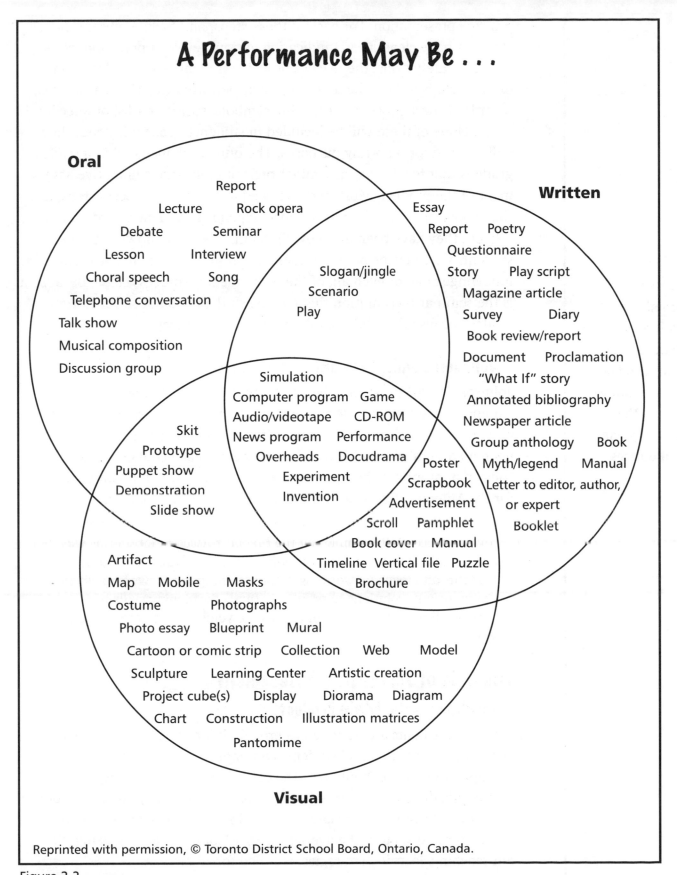

**Oral**

Report
Lecture      Rock opera
Debate      Seminar
Lesson      Interview
Choral speech      Song
Telephone conversation
Talk show
Musical composition
Discussion group

Slogan/jingle
Scenario
Play

**Written**

Essay
Report      Poetry
Questionnaire
Story      Play script
Magazine article
Survey      Diary
Book review/report
Document      Proclamation
"What If" story
Annotated bibliography
Newspaper article
Group anthology      Book
Myth/legend      Manual
Letter to editor, author,
or expert
Booklet

Skit
Prototype
Puppet show
Demonstration
Slide show

Simulation
Computer program      Game
Audio/videotape      CD-ROM
News program      Performance
Overheads      Docudrama
Experiment
Invention

Poster
Scrapbook
Advertisement
Scroll      Pamphlet
Book cover      Manual
Timeline  Vertical file  Puzzle
Brochure

Artifact
Map      Mobile      Masks
Costume      Photographs
Photo essay      Blueprint      Mural
Cartoon or comic strip      Collection      Web      Model
Sculpture      Learning Center      Artistic creation
Project cube(s)      Display      Diorama      Diagram
Chart      Construction      Illustration matrices
Pantomime

**Visual**

Figure 2.2

SkyLight Training and Publishing Inc

practice presentation. For each of these steps, and for the presentation, students have clear criteria indicating various levels of performance. As with the safety skills, the teacher provides students with feedback on each of these steps to help them develop their performance. The teacher keeps records of these process steps, using symbols, scores, marks, or anecdotal notes. None of these will be included in students' grades; instead, they will be used for reporting purposes. The only mark included in a student grade is that for the actual seminar presentation—the summative assessment of the product. Most students need to follow the process steps, and the quality of their final performance depends to a great extent on how diligent they have been in following them. There are, however, some students who may be able to present a high-quality seminar without following some, or even all, of the recommended process steps. Because it is the seminar presentation that counts, students do not suffer lower grades because they did not follow the suggested steps.

## Johnson's Mileposts and Checkpoints

Johnson (1996) provided labels for planned use of formative and summative assessment. He says we should consider assessments as *mileposts* (summative) or as *checkpoints* (formative). He suggested that teachers plan a number of milepost assessments for each course and then "design appropriate checkpoints—those activities which prepare students for the Milepost Assessment" (23). He goes on to say that checkpoints

> allow both the teachers and students to gauge a student's progress toward successfully completing the Milepost Assessment. In this way, curriculum, instruction, and assessment are all of the same cloth; students and teachers work together, searching for answers to essential questions, solutions to problems, [and] developing skills to apply—all the while using content as the vehicle which drives the work. (24)

## The Role of Formative Assessment
### Feedback—the Main Product

Many assessments are designed to provide information so that teachers can adjust instruction and students can improve performance. For example, this is—or should be—the prime purpose of quizzes; teachers give a quiz during the instructional process to see how students are doing with their learning; if the class average is 90%, the teacher knows to move on rapidly, but if the average is 30%, some reteaching using different teaching/learning strategies, is called for.

**Many assessments are designed to provide information so that teachers can adjust instruction and students can improve performance. This should be the prime purpose of quizzes.**

Similarly, individual students are informed on how they are doing and so can act appropriately. The teacher, of course, also uses information about individual students for remediation or enrichment. The same considerations apply to teacher questions, most homework (Nottingham 1988, 27), many worksheets, most teacher observation, and initial student attempts at any activity, such as writing or constructing a map. Stiggins et al. suggested that we consider these as "learning activities and not as assessments per se" (1989, 8).

Stiggins et al.'s concept of distinguishing clearly between learning and assessment also applies to most assessments by peer and self. This information primarily improves learning and thus is considered as formative, not summative, assessment. Peer assessment and/or self-assessment are included in grades only when such assessment is a stated learning goal and when students have had many opportunities to practice it. Then, we know that the likelihood is high that their assessment will be of high quality.

## The Role of Coaching

In activities such as band and basketball, students understand that practice counts, not directly but indirectly. It is practice that makes the spring concert great or enables the team to make the playoffs. Because we put a mark that counts directly on everything students do in the classroom, we contradict the value that practice usually represents to students. Coaching of the type that we see in band and basketball is needed in the classroom. It will not be easy, but, through an educative process, students may again understand that doing worksheets, doing their homework, and trying their best on quizzes that do not count directly in their grade is practice and will lead to much better performance on the summative assessments that do count in grades. (Note that, for those students who do well on formative assessments and not as well on summative assessments, the concerns addressed in Chapters 3 and 5 need to be carefully considered.)

## Feedback as Motivation

A benefit to students from feedback is it can be very motivational. After a score of 7 out of 10 has been put on a small assignment, there is not much more that can be said; rather, if teachers indicate one or two strengths and one or two weaknesses, they have the basis for discussions with individual students to help them improve their work. The basic

**Coaching of the type that we see in band and basketball is needed in the classroom.**

principle at work here is that words open up communication, whereas numbers close it down—and prematurely at that.

## Marking Quantity

A very common complaint of teachers at all levels is that they have too much marking. This is often true—because they mark too much! It is not necessary, from a measurement point of view, to mark everything students do. Assessment can be reliable as long as there are several samples of each type of work from each student.

Marking everything is also not necessary from an educational point of view. Teachers claim they must mark everything so that students will do the work. But, as has been indicated, this does not provide good information to students and, according to many experiments, damages motivation (Kohn 1993b, 47). Brookhart said that "the more feedback helps students view a grade as their own responsibility and as amenable to sustained and consistent effort, the more they will see school achievement as having an internal locus and being stable and controllable" (1994, 294). A much better approach, thus, is for teachers to check students' work regularly without always providing marks. This lightens a teacher's workload in a number of ways:

- Some work can simply be recorded as done or not done.

- Some work, for example, first drafts in creative writing, can be skimmed for a general overall impression rather than examined for the detail that is necessary to arrive at a score.

- Some work may be assessed by focusing on one or two key characteristics rather than everything. Strengths and weaknesses in essential aspects can be identified clearly in this approach.

Each of these approaches saves time—and is more beneficial to students—compared to marking everything, because most teachers are very conscientious when marking work that will be included in student grades. As Chapman said, ". . . daily quizzes, interim tasks, single journal entries and other contributing pieces and checks for understanding may merit a + or a – mark, but don't merit intense bean counting. Because teachers are not accountants, it is not helpful if they have to spend long hours entering a [mark] for every classroom activity" (1993, 222).

## The Role of Mistakes

A very important concept that is also honored by this guideline is the idea that mistakes are our friends. Spady noted that mistakes are "inherent elements in the journey toward learning competence" (1987, 11). The problem with including everything, he stated, is that grades "label those mistakes failures and make their consequences *irreversible*, [which] is counter to the notion of human growth and our inherent potential for change and improvement" (1987, 11).

## Concern About Excluding Formative Assessment Scores

It is very important to emphasize that excluding formative assessment scores from grades does not mean that they are unimportant. Formative assessments are critical to the learning process, because, as Airasian said, "they provide feedback when it is still possible to influence the process, and are at the heart of teaching" (1994, 136). Teachers must emphasize this to students and to parents to develop a new understanding of what counts. It is essential that teachers know which students are doing well and which are not. This knowledge lets all concerned build on the strengths and correct the weaknesses of individual students.

**Excluding formative assessment scores from grades does not mean that they are unimportant.**

# The Role of Summative Assessment
## Performance—Data Source for Grades

What does count for grades are the performances that students give to demonstrate the knowledge, skills, and behaviors they have acquired as the result of instruction and practice. These demonstrations usually occur at the end (however arbitrarily the end is defined) of a unit, a course, or a grading period.

## Variety of Summative Assessments

This guideline does not emphasize just exams and unit tests. There are many possible summative assessments, especially if performance assessment is used. See Figure 2.2. For most subjects, a combination of assessment types may be used: paper-and-pencil tests—primarily for knowledge; performance assessment—primarily for application of knowledge and to recognize skills and behaviors; and personal communication—to evaluate aspects of all types of learning goals.

A good example of varied summative assessments are those that are done before one can obtain a driver's license. First, there is usually a written test on the rules of the road and common driving situations. This is often followed by an eye test, and finally, there is a performance assessment of the critical skill—driving. Student drivers must pass all three tests to obtain a license. This model may be applied in the classroom when we want students to demonstrate their knowledge, skills, and behaviors.

(It is also worth noting that most people take lessons and practice for a long time before they try the driving test. While they are doing this, the instructor provides them with feedback. Also note that instructors do not give each lesson a mark to be factored in with the score on the driving test that determines if the license will the issued!)

**Give students opportunities to practice before undertaking assessments that count directly in grades.**

It must be emphasized again that Guideline 2 supports learning and encourages student success by giving students opportunities to practice before undertaking assessments that count directly in grades. In this regard, there are two critical points. First, it is critical not only that students have opportunities to practice their knowledge, skills, and behaviors, but also that they have opportunities to practice the type of assessment that is to be used summatively before a summative assessment is made. Second, it is also critical that more than one assessment method be used. This ensures comprehensive and consistent indications of student performance (Rogers and Graham 1997). Travis supported this viewpoint and suggested that it "is especially true when the educator wants to take varying learning styles and strategies into consideration" (1996, 309). This principle is being applied in school districts that are using the "bodies of evidence" concept. The school district of Aurora, Colorado, for example, requires that validation of competency on each of their district standards must involve several assessments, at least one of which must be a performance assessment. A superb analysis of formative and summative assessment and their roles in learning can be found in Harlen and James (1997).

## What's the Bottom Line?

What should be in grades?—scores from summative assessments. What should not be in grades?—scores from formative assessments.

The practical implication of Guideline 2 is that teachers should have in their grade books a page for reporting purposes, the formative page, and a page for grading, the summative page.

# What's My Thinking Now?

Analyze Guideline 2 for grading  (Sample student performance . . . ) by focusing on the following three questions:

Why use it?

Why not use it?

Points of  uncertainty

After careful thought about these points, answer these two questions:

Would I use Guideline 2 now?

Do I agree or disagree with the guideline, or am I unsure at this time?

(See the following for one person's reflections on Guideline 2.)

# A Reflection on Guideline 2

## WHY USE IT?

- feedback allows students to improve performance

- reduces marking load

- encourages both practice and risk taking

- allows for remedial instruction, intervention, and self-assessment

- encourages competency/mastery

## WHY NOT USE IT?

- some students, if not rewarded by grades, will not work

- fewer marks in grades makes grades less reliable

- effect on motivation

- penalizes early success

- students not mature enough to value feedback without marks/grades

## POINTS OF UNCERTAINTY

- how to select what goes in a grade and what doesn't

- what balance is there between formative and summative

- can students get over the "does-it-count?" syndrome?

- role/place of quizzes

- students want pay to equal grades in order to work

SkyLight Training and Publishing Inc

**CHAPTER 3**

# CHANGING GRADES

*If students demonstrate achievement at any time that, in effect,*

*renders past assessment information inaccurate, then you must drop*

*the former assessment from the record and replace it with the new.*

*To do otherwise is to misrepresent that achievement.*

—Stiggins (1997, 431)

| GUIDELINE | **Grade in pencil—keep** |
|:---:|:---:|
| **3** | **records so they may** |
|  | **be updated easily.** |

## The Case of Anil's Amazing Improvement

Anil enrolled in a Grade 9 keyboarding course for one semester. He has never had a computer or a typewriter at home and has had very limited keyboarding opportunities in the schools he attended previously. He chose to take keyboarding because he realized that, in senior high school courses and in college, he would be required to write essays and term papers that teachers would prefer (or require) to be typed. He was, therefore, highly motivated to succeed. He was fortunate also that he had been assigned to Mr. Smith's class. Mr. Smith was an excellent teacher who had great ability in identifying student strengths and weaknesses in keyboarding and in providing appropriate activities to maximize student progress.

As would be expected, Anil did not do very well in the first few weeks—his technique was poor, his speed was slow, and he made many errors—especially as compared with the other students, most of whom had considerable experience with computers, both at home and in their previous schools. Most of Anil's marks in the first six-week grading period were between 40% and 60%, so on the first report he had a grade of 50%. In the second grading period, Anil improved significantly and most of his marks were between 60% and 80%—his grade for this period was 70%. In the third grading period, it all came together for Anil—the combination of Mr. Smith's excellent teaching and Anil's motivation resulted in marks of 90% to 100% on every project and skill. However, the night before the final exam, Anil's parents told him that they were going to separate. Not surprisingly, he did not do very well on the final exam, receiving a mark of only 60%. When combined with his term work for the third grading period, his grade was 81%! School policy required that the grades for the three grading periods be averaged, thus, Anil's final grade was only 68%. Anil had clearly mastered keyboarding but, because marks for his early work were included and another assessment opportunity was not provided for the final exam, on which he scored lower than his demonstrated skill, his final grade did not reflect fairly his achievement in keyboarding.

# What's the Purpose of the Guideline?

This guideline supports learning by acknowledging that learning is an ongoing process and that what matters is how much learning occurs, not when it occurs. We take courses to learn, and what we did not know at the beginning should not be held against us. We also need to honor individual differences by recognizing that students learn at different rates and do not always perform at their real level on their first attempt, in a set time, or on one method of assessment.

# What Are the Key Elements of the Guideline?

The principles involved in this guideline can also be effectively illustrated by the process by which new drivers are accredited in Canada. Driving competence requires both knowledge and skills, and these are usually assessed, respectively, by a selected response test and a performance assessment. The process is multiphased. First, students learn about the rules of the road and other aspects of driving on their own. When they believe they are ready, they present themselves for the written test. If their judgment is wrong and they do not pass the written test, they may study more and take the test again (and again and again, if necessary!). There are costs associated with this—certainly time and usually money—but each test experience is separate. Their efforts on second (or later) tests are not averaged with their previous scores.

Second, after passing the written test, aspiring drivers move on to driving lessons. Most struggle at the beginning, but with good instruction and good feedback (formative assessment), they progress; they do not, however, receive marks for each lesson! When their instructor believes they are ready for the driving examination, they present themselves at the Test Center. (As the instructor has no marks for each student, these cannot be provided to the assessor to average with their performance on the exam.) The student then attempts the driving exam: many pass on their first attempt, but many (including the author) fail on their first attempt. When this happens, most aspiring drivers practice very hard on their deficiencies and, when ready, attempt the exam again. When they present themselves at the Test Center, the assessor, who does not know or, for that matter care, that they failed the first (or previous) time(s), does not

**What matters is how much learning occurs, not when it occurs.**

average their performances with previous attempts. If the student driver meets the standard on the test this time, he or she passes and receives his or her license.

In both the written and performance assessments, the assessor uses the most recent information, and the opportunity exists for more than one attempt at each assessment. It is important to note that the fact that a driver made more than one attempt at either part of the test does not appear on the license!

There are obvious differences between obtaining a driver's license and what happens in schools. Time is the most significant difference: schooling is generally defined by the calendar, whereas obtaining a driver's license is not. There are, however, many similarities, especially the emphasis on combining knowledge and skills to demonstrate competence. Thus, the principles involved in testing new drivers can be applied to a considerable extent in classroom assessment.

## Use the Most Recent Information

> If a kid falls head over heels in love and flunks the first math chapter test (getting 15 out of 100), and gradually over the term comes up to 95 out of 100, the grade the kid gets is going to be a C–. How long is he or she going to pay for that 15? And does the C– really show what the kid knows? (Hart 1996, 60)

> . . . the key question is, "What information provides the most accurate description of students' learning at this time?" In nearly all cases the answer is "The most current information." If students demonstrate that past assessment information no longer accurately reflects their learning, that information must be dropped and replaced by the new information. Continuing to rely on past assessment data miscommunicates students' learning. (Guskey 1996, 21)

These quotes demonstrate very clearly the reasons why teachers should "keep records so they may be updated easily." The suggestion that teachers should grade in pencil is somewhat symbolic; but it is a fact that it is easier to use the most recent information and do the necessary updating of records if the records are entered using a pencil—and, it is suggested, one that has an eraser! What is really important is not the method of recording but the mindset that acknowledges that, for knowledge or skills that are in any way cumulative or repetitive, teachers need to look at the most recent information to determine grades.

**To assess knowledge or skills that are in any way cumulative or repetitive, teachers need to look at the most recent information to determine grades.**

## Suitability for Different Grade Levels

Another way to say this is that teachers should base grades on the highest, most consistent level of performance, not the whole range of performance. This obviously applies in the previous examples—keyboarding and driving—but it has broad application in elementary schools, where we often see rapid development in student knowledge and skills over the course of the school year. This is especially true in the early grades. Using the most recent information is essential because of the varied and often rapid development of skills and abilities in young learners. Teachers sometimes attach first month and last month writing samples to final report cards; for most early-year students, the differences are immense. When rapid development is taking place, to base grades in any way on first-month work would obviously be wrong.

In middle school, high school, and college, basing grades on recent performance applies to some extent in most subjects, but is probably most obvious in modern languages, mathematics, writing, drama, and other courses that emphasize skill development and/or performance.

## Relationship to Improvement Grading

Some may see this guideline as an endorsement for what is often called "improvement grading." It very definitely is not. Advocates of improvement grading, such as MacIver and Reuman (1993/94), support involved mathematical calculation of improvement scores because they believe that this approach is most effective in motivating students to work hard. Although there may be some truth in this, there are two major problems with improvement grades—particularly if we want the primary purpose of grades to be to communicate student achievement as accurately as possible. First, improvement grades distort achievement by factoring in scores for improvement rather than just achievement. The distortion is particularly severe for students at the top and bottom ends of the achievement scale. Those at the top end find it very difficult to obtain improvement points because they have little room to improve, whereas those at the bottom end may obtain many improvement points, which have the effect of distorting their achievement by communicating that it is much greater than it really is.

Second, it is much better to simply use the most recent information; students then get full credit for their improvement rather than a score based on artificial manipulation of numbers. We are able to focus on

> **Teachers should base grades on the highest, most consistent level of performance, not the whole range of performance.**

grading as an exercise in professional judgment, rather than as an exercise in mechanical number crunching.

Improvement is best considered as a reporting variable and not primarily as a grading variable. Grades then are based on the students' highest, most consistent level of performance, which will usually be their most recent performance.

### Reflecting on . . . a Sample Grading Inventory

Consider the following grading inventory that has been adapted from a real high school example.

**GRADING INVENTORY FOR GRADE 9 KEYBOARDING**

| Components | First Grading Period % | Second Grading Period % | Third Grading Period % |
|---|---|---|---|
| Skill development including technique and warm up drills | 40 | 25 | 10 |
| Speed and Accuracy | 0 | 10 | 20 |
| Notebook | 10 | 10 | 10 |
| Tests and Assignments | 30 | 25 | 50 |
| Business Habits (including attendance, punctuality, preparedness for class, cooperation) | 20 | 10 | 10 |
| Exam | 0 | 20 | 0 |

The final grade is calculated by averaging the grades from each grading period. A final exam must be taken if a student has not received a grade of 70% in each grading period and/or has not met the school's attendance requirements. If the final exam is taken, it counts for 40% of the final grade with the grade for each grading period counting for 20%.

1. What problems do you see with this grading inventory?
2. What changes would you make to the grading inventory to make it consistent with Guideline 3?

## Provide Several Assessment Opportunities

This guideline acknowledges individual differences in many aspects of education, especially in planning teaching/learning strategies, and recognizes that life is full of second chances. The practical application of these principles is that, as much as possible, we must offer students varied assessment opportunities to support learning and encourage student success.

**Offer students varied assessment opportunities to support learning and encourage student success.**

## Individual Differences

Students learn at different rates and are able to demonstrate their knowledge and skills in different ways and at different speeds. This is part of our acknowledgment of individual differences, which encompass such specific concepts as learning styles and multiple intelligences as well as a more general understanding that students are different in many ways. As we acknowledge differences in learning, it is logical—and critical—that we provide varied opportunities for students to demonstrate their knowledge and skills.

## Second Chances

In the real world, very little of consequence depends on a single opportunity for performance. Most performances are practiced several times before they become real—think about writing, theater, and film just to name a few. In each of these fields, and many others, there is a great deal of assessment and redoing before a final product is released. Also, individuals are not evaluated on one piece of writing or one film; judgment of their quality as a performer is made over a body of work. This is also true in sports—individuals get many chances within each game to improve their performance, and teams have multiple opportunities to improve their performance because they play many games over the course of a season.

**As life provides second (and more) chances, so should school.**

As life provides second (and more) chances, so should school. There are many reasons why a student may not perform at their best on the day designated by a teacher for a test or performance. These may relate to learning, physical, or emotional factors. The objective of teachers is to identify the highest, most consistent level of performance of students; to do this, teachers need to vary assessment in many ways, including the number of opportunities, time available, and the methods used.

Guskey, quoted in the *ASCD Education Update,* puts it this way:

> . . . they have to have a second chance. What happens if a kid doesn't do well on this assessment? To me that says just as much about our teaching as it does about the skills and talents of that individual. And so for that individual, I have to find other ways of approaching (his) learning (and assessment) to help (him) learn those things well. (Grading performance assessments 1996, 5)

A number of opportunities at the same test can be provided by assessing the same concepts and skills using different questions and/or tasks. One potential major problem is unreasonable extra work for teachers; to avoid this, use computers to collect banks of items and tasks. This can be done at the school, district, and/or state level. Examples of this approach are being provided by the Maryland Assessment Consortium and by the Center on Learning, Assessment, and School Structure (CLASS).

Baron and Boschee went as far as to say that "students failing to successfully complete all secured tasks (i.e., assessment of individual student's work under controlled conditions) during the course of the academic year should be provided with an opportunity to demonstrate an acceptable level on each unsuccessful task prior to the end of the year" (1995, 78). This would obviously be logistically difficult, but it has implications that teachers need to consider for so-called final examinations.

An interesting variation of this idea was presented by Busick and Stiggins. They described a school district whose policy required that "incompletes" be given before students failed so that students had extended opportunities to complete missing work. The policy, however, created many problems, which Busick and Stiggins examined in a case study format (1997, 103–104).

The time available for students on any assessment, especially high stakes summative assessments, needs to be flexible. There are very few aspects of knowledge and skill that need to be demonstrated in a time-limited manner. In-class tests and formal examinations need to be conducted in a way that allows students considerable flexibility. Teachers recognize that different students process knowledge and skills at different rates—thus, it is important to measure the quality, not the speed, of the performance. Also, when assessments involve on-demand writing, the speed at which individuals write is an important factor. Some students can fill a page in a minute whereas other students who know and understand just as well—or better—may take three or four minutes.

Although there may be logistical difficulties because of a school's timetable or exam timetable, there are many ways in which flexibility can be provided. In-class tests can be planned for significantly less time than the length of the class. One math teacher known to the author uses this approach in a 76-minute period: 10 minutes review; 50 minute test; and 16 minutes flex time—students may continue working on the test or do other work.

**There are very few aspects of knowledge and skill that need to be demonstrated in a time-limited manner.**

Another approach can be used if a school has a rotating timetable. Schedule tests when the class occurs in the period immediately before lunch or in the last period of the day, thus providing automatic flex time. For formal examinations, when there is a school-wide schedule, exam lengths could be set with a plus or minus factor of, say, one third. For example, for 90-minute exams, students would have up to 2 hours, whereas for 2-hour exams, students would have an additional 40 minutes available to them. This not only provides some flexibility but also allows an exam schedule with two or three exams per day. Both examples allow exams to be held at 9:00 a.m. and 1:00 p.m. Although it is not a desirable practice, if schools need to have three exams per day, most exams would be 90 minutes with the longer exams scheduled for the last time period. For example, exams would start at 9:00, 11:30, and 2:00 p.m., with any 2-hour exams starting at 2:00 p.m.

For schools on a block schedule, a very educationally appropriate but rather radical approach is to have a four-day exam schedule with one day designated for each period. In this type of schedule, no time limit needs to be set on any exam as each teacher has the whole day to assess students. This type of schedule eliminates common exams, for example, for Grade 9 math classes, but it also means that teachers have great flexibility with regard to their methods of assessment. These can range from traditional paper and pencil exams to individual oral exams or performance assessments. If teachers/schools believe strongly in the need for common exams, modify the above schedule so that the designated-day schedule is used for most subjects in the mornings with the afternoons being set aside for common exams—or vice versa.

It is very important to emphasize that, in all these situations, flexible time is provided to allow all students to demonstrate what they know and are able to do. Teachers professionally plan tests/exams for the stated time, not for the flexible time. A 90-minute exam would be planned in the belief that most students will be able comfortably to complete the exam in that time. The flex time is not designed as a safety net for teachers who create exams that are too long; it is designed to assist those students who need extra time to show what they know and can do.

Another important point about flexible time is that it must be available to all students, not just to those who have been identified as having special needs in one or more areas.

**In all these situations, flexible time is provided to allow all students to demonstrate what they know and are able to do.**

The methods used to assess students need to be varied. Not all students can demonstrate their knowledge and skills in a written format, so students require a variety of ways to demonstrate their achievement. More is said about this in Chapter 7.

Having provided a number of suggestions for how students can be provided with flexible assessments, it is now time for a qualifier. Second or multiple chance assessment does not mean an endless set of opportunities for students. This would be unrealistic and would place far too great a burden on teachers. As Ebert said, ". . . second chances do not just appear, nor do they naturally work out without some evidence (of students) using past mistakes to enhance future success. Therefore, reassessment is the opportunity and students learn the responsibility" (1992, 32).

There are practical implications from Ebert's remark:

1. Any reteaching, review, or reassessment is at the teacher's convenience.

2. Students provide some evidence that they have completed some "correctives" (Ebert 1992, 32) before they are allowed a reassessment opportunity. Correctives may include personal study/ practice, peer tutoring, worksheets, review classes, and so forth.

These views on the responsibility of students and the role of teachers are supported by Stiggins. He said that

> learning requires a collaborative partnership, with both partners fulfilling their part of their bargain. . . . As a teacher you must set limits on your contribution. . . . . let's say a student . . . performs poorly on [an] assessment that counts for a grade. As a teacher how do you respond? One option is to say "I told you so" and let it go. Another response is, . . . "I value your learning whenever it occurs. Do you want to practice now and redo the assessment? If you do, I will reevaluate your performance—no penalties. But the reevaluation will need to fit into my schedule." (1997, 426)

Correctives and reassessment opportunities can usually be organized somewhat informally, but if teachers want to provide these opportunities with a clear structure, Figure 3.1 suggests a way to do it. Whatever approach is used, it is critical that reassessment opportunities be available to all students. Although the main purpose of second chance assessment is to help students who have not performed

**Second or multiple chance assessment does not mean an endless set of opportunities for students.**

Date: _____

To the parents/guardians of _____

This is to inform you that your child is experiencing difficulties in
_____.
His/her latest test/assessment mark: _____. Teacher: _____

To help your child acquire and improve her/his knowledge and/or skills, a re-teach and review session of 40 minutes is offered _____(day)_____ after school. A re-testing will be offered _____(next day)_____ after school. Please make sure that your child makes good use of this opportunity. It will not be possible to change the time to accommodate everyone's schedule.

If there is a problem concerning your child's progress, please phone 111-1111 to speak to your child's teacher or the department head/chairperson.

Please sign the form to acknowledge that you have been notified about the re-teaching and re-testing opportunity for your child.

Signature of parent/guardian _____ Date: _____

Please return this form to your child's teacher immediately.

Adapted from a letter used by the Mathematics Department at Midland Avenue Collegiate Institute, Scarborough, Ontario, Canada.

[Author's Note: This letter focuses on students experiencing difficulties. The re-teach and review sessions and the re-testing schedule should, however, be available to all students.]

Figure 3.1

well, in order to be fair and to be seen to be fair, it must be available to all students.

When second or multiple chance assessment opportunities are provided, please do not use the approach recommended by Spiegel, who suggested that students should be allowed "retakes" but that they should not receive "retake grades higher than C" (1991, 631). I strongly recommend instead that students should receive whatever mark they earn on the retake, assuming that the assessment used for the retake is a quality assessment and that it is available to all students who have provided evidence of having completed the necessary correctives. This retake score now represents their real level of performance and achievement and should not be averaged with previous performances or arbitrarily limited in any way.

Guideline 3 is designed to support learning and encourage student success by focusing on the most recent information and by having considerable flexibility in assessment with regard to the number of opportunities, the time, and the methods that students have to demonstrate their knowledge and skills. Teachers, when acknowledging that students are different, also acknowledge that, in assessment, one size does not fit all.

## What's the Bottom Line?

Change grades when new (i.e., more recent) information provides a fairer picture of student achievement or when students are given second (or more) chances by having additional opportunities, more time, and varied methods of assessment.

The practical implication of this guideline is that teachers need to keep their records—either on paper or on a computer—in ways that may easily be changed or updated. "Grade in pencil" may not always be literal advice, but it needs to be the mindset that teachers have about recording grades.

**"Grade in pencil" may not always be literal advice, but it needs to be the mindset that teachers have.**

# What's My Thinking Now?

Analyze Guideline 3 (Grade in pencil—keep records so they may be updated easily) for grading by focusing on three questions:

Why use it?

Why not use it?

Points of uncertainty

After careful thought about these points, answer these two questions:

Would I use Guideline 3 now?

Do I agree or disagree with the guideline, or am I unsure at this time?

(See the following for one person's reflections on Guideline 3.)

# A Reflection on Guideline 3

*WHY USE IT?*

- success at the end is what counts
- promotes and rewards progress
- learning is not a race
- computer grade programs make it easy to grade in pencil
- extent to which learning goal achieved is more important than when it is achieved

*WHY NOT USE IT?*

- encourages "slackers" to wait until the last minute
- time constraints make reassessment impractical
- those who do best the first time usually do best later as well
- average of several attempts fairer than best score
- students can manipulate—play the system

*POINTS OF UNCERTAINTY*

- emphasis on process or product?
- effect on student motivation?
- transition into real world—second chances?
- is one student's third attempt a fair comparison with another's first attempt?
- reliability/validity of test items on second or third test?

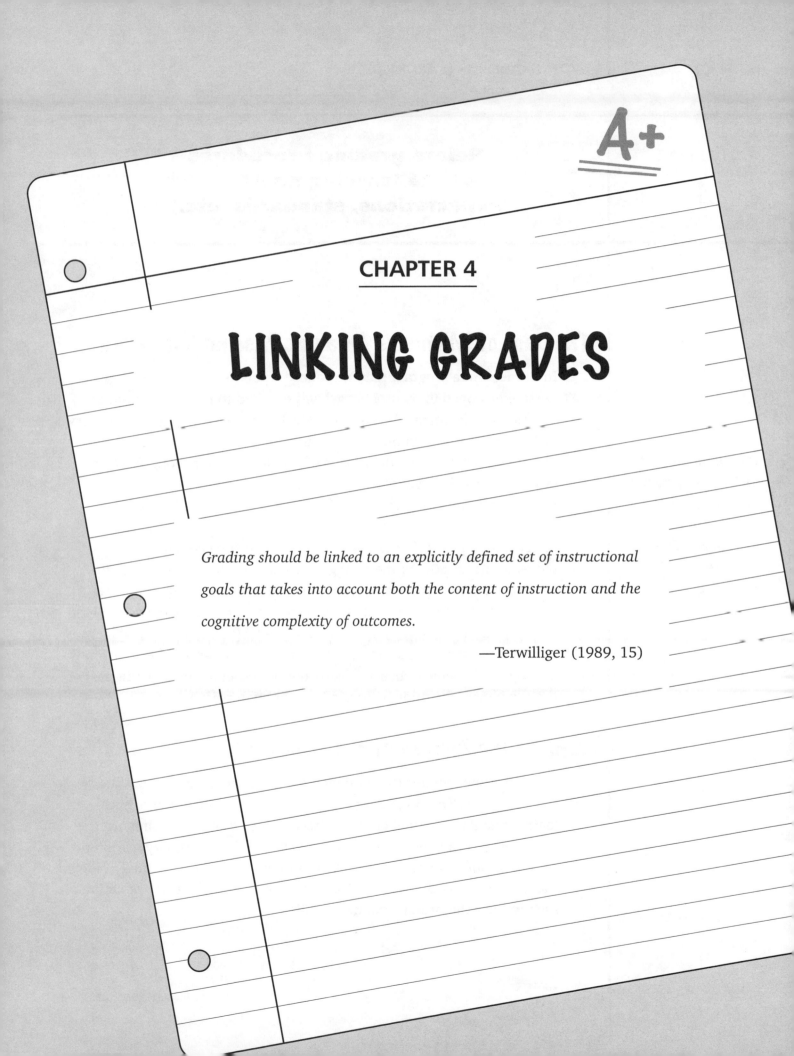

**CHAPTER 4**

# LINKING GRADES

*Grading should be linked to an explicitly defined set of instructional goals that takes into account both the content of instruction and the cognitive complexity of outcomes.*

—Terwilliger (1989, 15)

| GUIDELINE | **Relate grading procedures** |
|:---:|:---:|
| **4** | **to learning goals** |
| | **(expectations, standards, etc.).** |

The contribution of each learning goal to the final grade is directly proportional to its importance compared to other learning goals.

## The Case of Michael's Amazing Passing Shop Grade

In Grade 9, in a program that introduced students to the wide range of possibilities open to them, Michael was required to take a course in a vocational area. Michael chose Auto Mechanics, even though he had very little interest or skill in this area. During the six weeks of the class, he completed two poor quality repairs of simple problems, both of which deservedly received very low marks. School procedures established a highly structured assessment schedule, which provided four days of written exams at the middle and at the end of each semester. School policy also required that exams be held in each subject and that their scores count for 50% of the final grade. The Auto Mechanics exam included questions about safety procedures and how to make simple repairs. This assessment was easy for Michael because he had a good memory and wrote well. Michael received 50/50 on the exam, which was added to his performance marks. This combination resulted in an overall passing grade, which Michael clearly did not deserve, as the main goal of the course was for students to perform quality repairs.

## What's the Purpose of the Guideline?

This guideline requires that grading procedures be aligned with stated learning goals. This alignment is direct, and the contribution of each learning goal to the final grade is directly proportional to its importance compared to other learning goals. For example, if the primary learning goal in a course is practical demonstration of skills, then the final grade in that course is based on direct observation of those skills and evaluation of the products that result from those skills.

# What Are the Key Elements of the Guideline?

Most school districts and states/provinces now have clearly stated learning goals. Different words are used to describe these goals. In some places, outcomes is still the descriptor of choice, but in many places, other words, such as standards and expectations, have replaced it. It does not matter much which word is used; the concept is that at either the local or state level, specific learning targets have been established, often on a grade by grade basis. In this book, to simplify a confusing situation, I use *learning goals* as a generic term; however, when other sources are quoted, alternative terms to learning goals will be retained.

## Learning Goals

Grades should be effective communication vehicles, and the methods used to determine them need to provide optimum opportunities for student success and to encourage learning. For this to happen, the meaning of grades must be clear, which requires that, in addition to all the issues dealt with in Guidelines 1, 2, and 3, grades must be directly related to the learning goals for each grading period in each classroom. Teachers must understand clearly what learning results are expected and then base their grading plan (or inventory) on these learning goals.

> **Grades must be directly related to the learning goals for each grading period in each classroom.**

## Grading Inventories

### Off Target: Methods of Assessment

Before discussing an appropriate basis for a grading inventory, let's briefly discuss what not to use. Simply said, do not base a grading inventory on methods of assessment, as illustrated in Figure 4.1.

With this type of inventory, it is extremely difficult to appropriately emphasize each learning goal because the primary focus is on the methods of assessment. Each learning goal may be assessed in a number of ways, for example, there may be questions on tests/exams, written assignments, and demonstrations for each goal; but to align assessment with the desired emphasis on each goal over several methods of assessment is extremely difficult.

### On Target: Learning Goals

A much better approach is to develop a grading inventory with the learning goals as the components of grades. In this approach, the proportion of

# Traditional Inventory for Middle School Grading

| Evaluation Category | Expected Range |
|---|---|
| 1. Quizzes/tests/exams | 20–30% |
| 2. Written assignments<br>creative or explanatory paragraphs, essays, notes,<br>organizers, writing folios, portfolios | 15–25% |
| 3. Oral presentations or demonstrations<br>brief or more formal presentations or demonstrations,<br>role-playing, debates, skits, etc. | 15–25% |
| 4. Projects/assignments<br>research tasks, hands-on projects, video- or audiotaped<br>productions, analysis of issues, etc. | 10–20% |
| 5. Cooperative group learning<br>evaluation of the process and skills learned as an<br>individual and as a group member | 5–15% |
| 6. Independent learning<br>individual organizational skills, contributions to<br>class activities and discussions, homework, notebooks | 5–15% |
| | 70–130% |

Note: Aspects of this inventory conflict with other grading guidelines in addition to Guideline 4.

Figure 4.1

the total grade to be allocated to each learning goal is based on the importance of each learning goal in each grading period. This priority can be determined by teachers working collaboratively; for example, all the Grade 3 teachers in a school or all the Grade 9 science teachers meet to discuss and allocate goal importance and weight for each grading period. Discussions of this allocation may be the best professional dialogue teachers engage in because they have to be very clear about which goals are important at which point in the school year and they have to be prepared to support their own views while respecting the opinions of others. Another very important benefit of this approach is that there will be much greater consistency across a school than occurs with traditional, largely private, approaches to grading. The result of these discussions is an inventory like the one shown in Figure 4.2.

## Grading Inventory for Grade 9 Social Studies

| Items Included in Grades | Percentages Allocated | | |
|---|---|---|---|
| | Grading Period 1 | Grading Period 2 | Grading Period 3 |
| 1. Knowledge of key facts | 50 | 20 | 0 |
| 2. Understanding of basic concepts | 10 | 40 | 20 |
| 3. Identifies and explains causes, nature, and impact of local and national issues | 0 | 0 | 40 |
| 4. Applies social studies learning to life | 0 | 0 | 10 |
| 5. Communicates effectively | 20 | 20 | 10 |
| 6. Gathers, selects, and records information from a variety of sources | 20 | 10 | 0 |
| 7. Analyses and evaluates information from a variety of sources | 0 | 0 | 20 |
| 8. Cooperative learning skills | 0 | 10 | 0 |

Learning goals or items listed above are adapted from K–9 Outcomes for Geography and History, Scarborough Board of Education, Ontario, Canada.

Figure 4.2

In this inventory, some learning goals (2 and 5) may be part of the grade in each grading period whereas others (3, 4, 7, and 8) may be part of the grade in only one grading period. The remaining learning goals (1 and 6) contribute to the grade in two of the three grading periods. For learning goals that are part of the grade in more than one grading period, different percentages occur in some grading periods to reflect the shifting emphasis on learning goals as the year progresses. It is also important to note that, while there are eight learning goals for the course, no more than five are included in the grading inventory for any one grading period. This is quite deliberate, as it is difficult for teachers and students to really focus on more than about five learning goals at any one time. This does not mean that the other three learning goals are totally ignored in each grading period; it simply means that they are not emphasized, and are, therefore, not part of the grade for that grading period.

A variation of this approach is shown in Figure 4.3. In this example, the same weighting is used for the whole year. It is clear, however, that grades—in a subject for which it has always been difficult to provide meaningful grades—are related directly to learning goals.

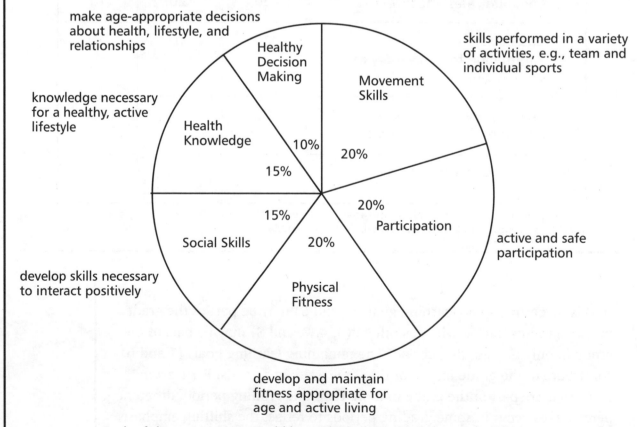

## Learning Goals Matched With Grading in Physical and Health Education, Grades 1–8

make age-appropriate decisions about health, lifestyle, and relationships

knowledge necessary for a healthy, active lifestyle

skills performed in a variety of activities, e.g., team and individual sports

Healthy Decision Making

Movement Skills

Health Knowledge

10%

20%

15%

20%

Participation

15%

Social Skills

20%

active and safe participation

develop skills necessary to interact positively

Physical Fitness

develop and maintain fitness appropriate for age and active living

Each of the components could be evaluated using rubrics or checklists.

Adapted from material developed by Carol Rocks, Curriculum Coordinator, Physical and Health Education, Scarborough Board of Education, Ontario, Canada.

Figure 4.3

SkyLight Training and Publishing Inc

## Sample Grade Book Extract

| Learning Goal | #1 | | | | #2 | | | | #3 | #4 | #5 | #6 | Grade Determination | | | | |
|---|---|---|---|---|---|---|---|---|---|---|---|---|---|---|---|---|---|
| Date | 9/15 | 9/22 | 9/22 | 9/24 | 9/29 | 9/30 | 10/1 | 10/2 | | | | | Highest Most Consistent Level of Performance | Total | Weighted Total | Mean | Median |
| Assessment Method | Debate | Collage | Quiz (F) | Homework (F) | Product | Performance | Quiz (F) | Test | | | | | | | | | |
| Scoring Method (see key) | S | R | 10 | C | R | R | 22 | % | | | | | | | | | |
| Student #1 | S | 4 | 7 | ✓ | 2 | 3 | 16 | 89 | | | | | | | | | |
| Student #2 | | | | | | | | | | | | | | | | | |
| Student #3 | | | | | | | | | | | | | | | | | |
| Student #4 | | | | | | | | | | | | | | | | | |
| Student #5 | | | | | | | | | | | | | | | | | |
| . | | | | | | | | | | | | | | | | | |
| . | | | | | | | | | | | | | | | | | |
| . | | | | | | | | | | | | | | | | | |
| Student #23 | | | | | | | | | | | | | | | | | |

**KEY**

R – Rubric Score
C – Completed ✓  Incomplete X
S – Another symbol system, e.g., S/U satisfactory/unsatisfactory
10 – total possible
% – marked out of 100
(F) – Formative-not included in grade

Figure 4.4

If grading inventories are approached in this fashion, the learning goals become the set and the assessment methods become the subset. Teachers identify for each assessment which components (or questions) fit with which learning goals and then record separate scores for each. A possible way in which to accomplish this is illustrated in Figure 4.4.

A detailed examination of this approach to grading is provided by Marzano and Kendall, who said that "first and foremost, the teacher must stop thinking in terms of assignments, tests and activities to which points are assigned, and start thinking in terms of levels of performance in the declarative and procedural knowledge specific to her subject area" (1996, 147). They also acknowledged that "the use of columns in a grade book to represent standards (learning goals), instead of assignments, tests and activities, is a major shift in thinking for teachers" (150).

Related issues raised by Marzano and Kendall are how scores are recorded, how final grades are calculated, and how student performances are reported. The first two issues are dealt with in Chapter 5, and the latter issue in Chapter 10. It is sufficient to note here with regard to

**The use of columns in a grade book to represent standards (learning goals), instead of assignments, tests and activities, is a major shift in thinking for teachers.** (Marzano and Kendall 1996, 150)

reporting that, if grades are related to learning goals it is, at the very least, highly desirable, if not essential, that report cards provide opportunities for teachers to provide specific information on each learning goal in addition to an overall grade.

## Establishing Scoring Criteria

There is another dimension of this guideline that needs to be considered. If grades are related to learning goals, it is critical that teachers mark each assessment on clear, pre-established criteria (targets, standards). The use of detailed rubrics or scoring guides is essential, and it is ideal to have students involved in the development of the rubrics or scoring guides (see Chapter 8).

**Students can hit any target they can see and which stands still for them.**

This is the complete opposite of the approach recommended by Mahon who said "teachers, like magicians are ill-advised to reveal too many tricks of the trade" (1996, 280). If we want grades with meaning and if we want assessment to contribute to learning, Mahon is wrong. As Stiggins says in almost every workshop he presents, "students can hit any target they can see and which stands still for them." But teachers have to provide this clarity and consistency in the form of rubrics and detailed scoring guides. Then students know what is expected and have some chance of producing it. Students also are able to use summative assessments to contribute to their growth by answering what Fogarty and Bellanca (1987, 227) called Mrs. Potter's Questions:

1. What were you expected to do?

2. In this assignment, what did you do well?

3. If you had to do this task over, what would you do differently?

4. What help do you need from me?

Clear criteria or targets also help us to deal with the issue of what grades mean because they provide "stable and clear points of reference," which Wiggins (1996, 142) said are often lacking but are necessary for symbols like grades to have meaning. An example of a rubric for expository writing (Figure 4.5) and a detailed scoring guide for a science experiment (Figure 4.6) are provided as examples for teachers to use in developing their own rubrics and scoring guides. Further useful information can be found in Danielson (1997), and discussion of the use of scoring guides and many sample scoring guides can be found in Pomperaug Regional School District 15 (1996).

# Expository Writing Assessment

Name _____     Date _____

Assignment _____

Assessor:     Teacher ☐     Peer ☐     Self ☐     Put a ✓ mark in the appropriate box for the level of performance for each criterion.

| Criteria for Expository Writing | Levels of Performance for Each Criterion | | | |
|---|---|---|---|---|
| | 1 | 2 | 3 | 4 |
| **Structure—introduction** means that the first sentence(s) clearly state the main idea(s) | The introduction is missing. | The introduction is included but is unclear or off topic. | The introduction is included but is somewhat unclear. | The introduction clearly states the main idea(s). |
| **Structure—conclusion** the last sentence(s) clearly summarize(s) the main idea(s) | The conclusion is missing. | The conclusion is included but is unclear or off topic. | The conclusion is included but is somewhat unclear. | The conclusion clearly summarizes the main idea(s). |
| **Supporting sentences, reasons or arguments** means that the sentences developing the main idea are clear and related to the main idea in a logical fashion | Supporting sentences, reasons, or arguments are mainly unclear and unconnected to the main idea. | Supporting sentences, reasons, or arguments are occasionally unclear and may be unconnected to the main idea or disorganized. | Supporting sentences, reasons, or arguments are usually clear and connected to the main idea in an organized way. | Supporting sentences, reasons, or arguments are always clear and connected to the main idea in an organized way. |
| **Evidence and examples** means the use of specific related facts, examples, or evidence to develop or support sentences, reasons, or arguments | No relevant, clear facts, examples, or evidence are given to support the arguments. | Some evidence is given as support. Many pieces of evidence are missing or irrelevant. | Most sentences, reasons, or arguments are developed or supported by relevant evidence and examples. | All sentences, reasons, or arguments are developed or supported by relevant evidence and examples. |
| **Mechanics of writing** means the use of correct spelling and grammar, such as sentence structure and proper wording | Major repeated errors in spelling and/or grammar. | Some significant errors in spelling and/or grammar. | Few significant errors in spelling and/or grammar. | No significant errors in spelling and grammar. |
| **Additional criteria** (developed by the teacher and students) | | | | |

**Comments and Suggestions for Improvement:**

Adapted with permission, ©Toronto District School Board, Ontario, Canada.

Figure 4.5

# Experiment Report

**Experiment Report**                                      Name(s): _____

_____

**Title Page**                                                                              /2
- title conveys information about experiment
- date investigation was performed                         _____
- name of person submitting report                         _____
- name of partners during investigation                    _____
                                                           _____

**Aim or Purpose**                                                                         /3
- describes 2 clear variables                              _____
- describes the situation in which the variables are being
  investigated – diagram can be used to illustrate situation  _____

**Equipment or Materials**                                                                 /3
- include name and model number                            _____

**Background & Theory**                                                                    /5
- reviewed concepts and theories used in the experiment    _____

**Procedure or Plan of Action**                                                            /12
- description of the equipment set-up (diagram)            _____
- described how to measure the independent variable        _____
- described how to measure the dependent variable          _____
- included an appropriate number of changes in the independent variable  _____
- included appropriate increments for the independent variable  _____
- described the other factors that may affect the results of the
  experiment and described how these factors were controlled  _____
- included appropriate repetition of trials                _____
- described steps clearly and in a logical order           _____

**Data and Observations**                                                                  /8
- recorded data or observations in an appropriate format   _____
- recorded an appropriate number of observations           _____
- recorded observations with proper accuracy               _____
- original record of observations present                  _____

**Calculations or Analysis**                                                               /11
- sample calculation included for repetitive calculations  _____
- an appropriate graph was drawn—grid lines included       _____
- appropriate LOBF was indicated                           _____
- analyzed graph—analysis and calculations done in order and with
  information statements to explain calculations
      trends                                               _____
      calculations including correct units and sig. digits _____

**Conclusion or Summary**                                                                  /7
- described the relationship between the variables including the
  equation derived from the graph if applicable            _____
- described any weaknesses in design or items that you didn't
  realize until after the experiment that would have affected the results  _____
- comparison with accepted theory                          _____

**Overall Appearance of the Report**                                                       /5
- neatness, order, organization
- correct use of grammar and spelling                      _____
- easy to read                                             _____
                                                           _____

**TOTAL**                                                                                  /56

Reproduced with the permission of the originator, Stephen Houlde, Science Department Head, Sir
Oliver Mowat Collegiate Institute, Scarborough, Ontario, Canada.

Figure 4.6

## Learning Goals and Passing Grades

The final issue that needs to be considered in connection with this guideline is whether students should be credited for a course if they have not demonstrated mastery of the critical learning goals. In the example in Figure 4.2, it would appear that the teachers considered one of the first three learning goals to be critical in each term because these goals accounted for 50%, or almost 50%, of the grade. Although unlikely, it would be possible for a student to obtain very low marks on these learning goals, while obtaining sufficiently high marks on the other six learning goals to obtain a passing grade. Teachers and schools need to decide if this is acceptable. If they really believe some learning goals are critical, then students will not obtain credit unless they have achieved a reasonable level of competence, ideally mastery, on those learning goals. If this approach is used, it obviously complicates the grading process, but it does support the concept that grading is an exercise in professional judgment, not just a mechanical, numerical exercise.

It also illustrates the interconnectedness of the grading guidelines because, for example, Guidelines 2 and 3 become absolutely critical. Formative assessment has to be used to provide information to students and teachers about progress (Guideline 2), and students need to have growth acknowledged appropriately and have varied opportunities to demonstrate competence (Guideline 3).

> **Grading is an exercise in professional judgment, not just a mechanical, numerical exercise.**

# What's the Bottom Line?

Link grades to these:

- learning goals (standards, expectations, outcomes, etc.), not assessment methods
- teachers' clear understanding of what learning results are expected
- marks obtained from assessments with clear criteria (rubrics, scoring guides)
- reporting that allows for detailed information on learning goals
- credits granted only when students have mastered the critical learning goals

This guideline has these practical implications:

- Teachers use grade books where the columns primarily represent the learning goals and secondarily represent assessment methods.

- Teachers and students develop rubrics or detailed scoring guides for all summative assessments included in grades.

- Teachers use an expanded format for reporting.

# What's My Thinking Now?

Analyze Guideline 4 for grading (Relate grading procedures to learning goals . . .) by focusing on three questions:

Why use it?

Why not use it?

Points of uncertainty

After careful thought about these points, answer these two questions:

Would I use Guideline 4 now?

Do I agree or disagree with the guideline, or am I unsure at this time?

(See the following for one person's reflections on Guideline 4.)

# A Reflection on Guideline 4

*WHY USE IT?*

- *realistically reflects intentions of course*
- *provides clear goal/focus*
- *students know why they received grade*
- *consistency and fairness*
- *makes teachers accountable*

*WHY NOT USE IT?*

- *loss of creativity*
- *too great a shift in thinking/practice*
- *learning goals often vague*
- *community reaction*
- *huge amount of work to define learning goals, develop standards, rubrics, etc.*

*POINTS OF UNCERTAINTY*

- *clarity of learning goals?*
- *fair to all learning styles?*
- *weighting learning goals?*
- *mastery or pass/fail?*
- *how many learning goals?*

**CHAPTER 5**

# CRUNCHING NUMBERS

*Grades based on averaging have meaning only when averaging repeated measures of similar content. Teachers average marks on fractions, word problems, geometry and addition with marks for attendance, homework and notebooks—and call it mathematics. In Mathematics we teach that you cannot average apples, oranges and bananas, but we do it in our grade books!*

—Canady, workshop, Association for Supervision and Curriculum Development Annual Meeting, April 1993

| GUIDELINE 5 | **Crunch numbers carefully.** |

Guideline 5 has teachers question the widely accepted practice of simply averaging marks to arrive at final grades.

## The Case of Alexis' Absences

Alexis was a brilliant Grade 11 student who received almost perfect marks on every summative assessment (tests, products, demonstrations, etc.) for which she was present—and she usually was present to take major tests/exams and to submit major assignments on the due dates. Alexis, however, missed many classes and often did not hand in required work (homework, first drafts, etc.). She also did not complete her notebook and, because of her absences and shy personality, her participation in class discussions was infrequent. As a result of these circumstances, there were always many zeros in teachers' grade books for Alexis—for missed quizzes, lab reports, small assignments, notebook, attendance, participation, and so forth. Alexis received a D in most subjects, and, because of her lack of success, she was considering dropping out. Alexis' low grades resulted from averaging her many zeros with her 90%+ scores, and clearly did not reflect her achievement. She was penalized over and over again for her poor attendance—which was caused by her single-parent father frequently requiring her to stay at home to look after her younger siblings!

## What's the Purpose of the Guideline?

This guideline supports learning and encourages student success by having teachers question the widely accepted practice of simply averaging marks to arrive at final grades. This questioning leads teachers to examine all aspects of number crunching, including weighting, that are involved in the calculation of grades.

## What Are the Key Elements of the Guideline?

Number crunching has been part of teachers' lives from the time grades were introduced. Discussion of each of the grading guidelines focuses on the idea that to have grades with meaning and to have grades that support learning, grading must be an exercise in professional judgment, rather than simply a mechanical, numerical exercise. However, it is realistic to recognize that some teachers see grading as primarily a number crunching exercise to fulfill the responsibilities imposed on them by their employment. Although such teachers will probably ignore the other guidelines and continue to do what they have always done, this guideline is critical for them because, at the very least, they need to examine their number crunching practices. For teachers who move toward grading as an exercise in professional judgment and apply one or more of the other guidelines, there will be varying degrees of involvement with number crunching, so this guideline remains important for them as well.

## Mean Versus Median

The average does not have to be the *mean*; consider using medians. Although both are measures of central tendency, a *mean* is the total of the values, divided by the number of values, whereas the *median* is the middle value of the data listed in numerical order. This aspect of Guideline 5 asks teachers to consider two dimensions of importance: (1) quantity or quality and (2) all or some evidence.

**The average does not have to be the mean; consider using medians.**

### Reflecting on . . . Problems With the Mean

|  | Karen | Alex | Jennifer | Stephen |
|---|---|---|---|---|
| Assessment #1 | 90 | 63 | 100 | 100 |
| Assessment #2 | 90 | 63 | 100 | 100 |
| Assessment #3 | 90 | 63 | 100 | 90 |
| Assessment #4 | 90 | 63 | 100 | 90 |
| Assessment #5 | 90 | 63 | 100 | 63 |
| Assessment #6 | 90 | 63 | 100 | 63 |
| Assessment #7 | 90 | 63 | 10 | 62 |
| Assessment #8 | 0 | 63 | 10 | 62 |
| Assessment #9 | 0 | 63 | 10 | 0 |
| Assessment #10 | 0 | 63 | 0 | 0 |
| Total | 630 | 630 | 630 | 630 |
| Mean | 63% | 63% | 63% | 63% |
| Median | 90% | 63% | 100% | 63% |

Study the information in the chart. Assume that these are the marks four students have received for ten summative assessments in a school subject—elementary, secondary, or college. What grade should each student receive?

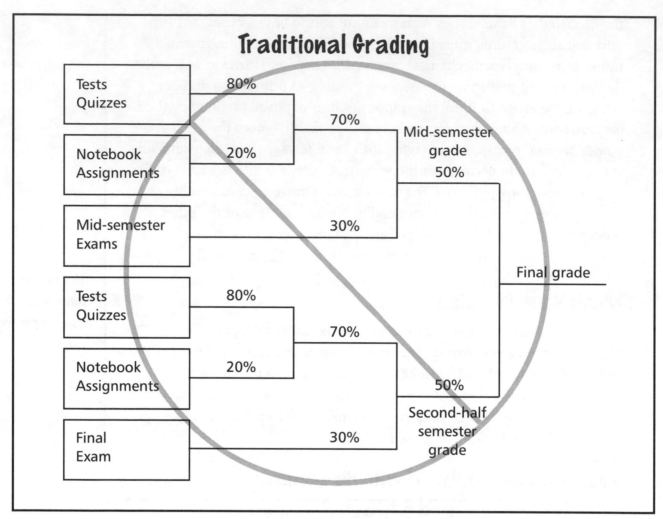

Figure 5.1

Note that all students received the same mean scores, but that the median scores for Karen and Jennifer are much higher. In schools using traditional grading schemes, such as the one illustrated in Figure 5.1, all four students would receive a grade of 63%, which would vary from a C to an F depending on the grading scale in use in the school, district, or college.

The traditional approach emphasizes quantity over quality and completing all work rather than doing some superbly and missing some. It is clear, however that the quality of the work, that is, the achievement of each student, is very different. Karen generally produced high quality work, but for some reason did not submit three of the ten summative assessments. Alex produced consistently mediocre work but submitted all the summative assessments. Jennifer produced superb work on six of the assessments, very poor work on three of the assessments, and did not submit one of the assessments. Stephen's performance was very inconsistent—four assessments were excellent, four were mediocre, and two were not submitted.

In deciding grades for these students, consider these statements by Guskey (1996):

> assigning a score of zero to work that is late or missed or neglected does not accurately depict student's learning. Is the teacher certain the student has learned absolutely nothing, or is the zero assigned to punish students for not displaying appropriate responsibility? (21)

> a zero has a profound effect when combined with the practice of averaging. Students who receive a single zero have little chance of success because such an extreme score skews the average. (21)

> Averaging falls far short of providing an accurate description of what students have learned. For example, students often say, "I have to get a B on the final to pass this course." But does this make sense? If a final examination is truly comprehensive and students' scores accurately reflect what they have learned, should a B level of performance translate to a D for the course grade? If the purpose of grading and reporting is to provide an accurate description of what students have learned, then *averaging must be considered inadequate and inappropriate.* (21)

Guskey's statements clarify the problem with using the mean, the most commonly used measure of central tendency: the mean always lets the bad overtake the good, so that for every low mark earned, a student needs many good marks to return to his or her real level. This is evident in the grades of Karen and Jennifer—most of their work is of a very high quality, but for some reason(s), they either did poorly or did not submit some of the assessments. This problem is compounded when teachers include zeros for behavioral reasons (attendance, tardiness, misconduct, etc).

## The Median Alternative

An alternative to using the mean is to use the median. Wright stated that teachers' marks are ordinal data (numbers on a scale whose intervals are uncertain or inconsistent) and that "the median is the statistically correct measure of central tendency for ordinal data" (1994, 724). This is the technical argument for using medians, but an equal or more important argument is the philosophical one. Wright advocates, and uses, medians in his college courses because they "provide more opportunities for success by diminishing the impact of a few stumbles and rewarding hard work" (723). Wright noted that everyone has days on which they do not produce their best work, and that everybody is not good at everything,

Medians "provide more opportunities for success by diminishing the impact of a few stumbles and rewarding hard work." (Wright 1994, 723)

## Computing a Median for One Student

| | Learning Goal #1 | L.G. #2 | L.G. #3 | L.G. #4 | L.G. #5 |
|---|---|---|---|---|---|
| Assessment #1 | 90 | 100 | 70 | 95 | 60 |
| Assessment #2 | 90 | 90 | 70 | 90 | 50 |
| Assessment #3 | 90 | 0 | 70 | 40 | 40 |
| Median | 90 | 90 | 70 | 90 | 50 |
| Mean | 90 | 63 | 70 | 75 | 50 |

Overall Median 90                    Overall Mean 70

Figure 5.2

**The use of the median has the greatest impact when performance is highly variable.**

but neither of these failings suggests that most of the time they do not produce high-quality work. The use of means emphasizes variability, whereas the use of medians reduces the impact of variability very dramatically.

In order to use medians, all scores have to be converted to a common scale (ideally, percentages). Then, calculate a median for all summative assessments used in a course (which, it is hoped, would not be many more than ten) or for each category if different categories are used. Next, also calculate a median among the categories to arrive at the final grade. (To be consistent with Guideline 4, the categories would be learning goals, not assessment methods.) See Figure 5.2 for an example of using medians.

It is obvious from the example in Figure 5.2 that the use of the median has the greatest impact when performance is highly variable. Thus, students who perform at a consistently high level or at a consistently low level would see little or no difference in their final grades regardless of which method of central tendency is used.

The problem with the use of medians for many teachers is their fear that it encourages students to play games and manipulate the system to their advantage by making minimal or no effort on some assessments. If this is (or becomes) a problem, it may be necessary to require that students submit/complete a certain percentage of assessments with a required minimal level of performance. It also may be necessary to designate some assessments as essential—this would mean that a mark would be included regardless of whether the assessment was completed and regardless of that method of calculation was used. However, if the median is used in association with the other guidelines, if students have a clear understanding of the supportive success orientation of the grading procedures being used, and if the students are presented with course material and assessments that are interesting and engaging, this should not be a problem.

The main purpose of grades is to communicate achievement. Regardless of which measure of central tendency is used, grades (symbols) need to be supplemented by as much information as possible. If medians are selected, it is particularly important that some form of expanded format reporting be used, so that a clear picture of performance can be given. For example, for the student in Figure 5.2, it would be very important to be able to report that her performance on learning goal #5 was weak.

In concluding discussion of this aspect of Guideline 5, it is important to note that it says only "consider using medians." Changing from the use of the mean would be a giant step for many teachers and many communities—for many, the step may be too large. At the very least, however, teachers need to consider the issues involved and devise better ways of dealing with work that is late, missing, or neglected, other than simply assigning zeros.

**Teachers need to devise better ways of dealing with work that is late, missing, or neglected, other than simply assigning zeros.**

# Weighting Marks

A second aspect of Guideline 5 is the necessity of weighting marks carefully to achieve intent in final grades. The way in which marks are combined generally involves varying the importance or weighting of the different learning goals and/or assessment methods. In Chapter 4, it was suggested that grading inventories need to be based primarily on learning goals rather than assessment methods. Regardless of which approach is used it is very important that weighting be done so the teacher's intent is achieved in the final grade.

## Use of a Common Scale

Using grade book software (see Chapter 9), it is relatively easy to ensure that the major components (learning goals or assessment methods) receive their intended weights. However, within each component, it is essential that the marks be included on a consistent or common scale. The easiest common scale to use is percentages: convert all marks to a

# Comparison of Grade Weighting Alternatives

| Scenario | Test | Performance |
|---|---|---|
| weight | 1 | 2 |
| point value | 40 | 20 |
| Amanda's scores | 10 | 20 |
| Alan's scores | 40 | 5 |

| Alternative | Amanda | Alan |
|---|---|---|
| 1. Apply weighting to raw scores | $\dfrac{(10 \times 1) + (20 \times 2)}{(40 \times 1) + (20 \times 2)} = \dfrac{50}{80} = 60\%$ | $\dfrac{(40 \times 1) + (5 \times 2)}{(40 \times 1) + (20 \times 2)} = \dfrac{50}{80} = 60\%$ |
| 2. Apply weighting to point values (i.e., test, 40 pts, performance, 80 pts) | $\dfrac{10 + 80}{40 + 80} = \dfrac{90}{120} = 75\%$ | $\dfrac{40 + 20}{40 + 80} = \dfrac{60}{120} = 50\%$ |
| 3. Apply weighting using a common scale (percentages) | $\dfrac{10}{40} = \dfrac{25 \times 1}{100 \times 1}$ <br> $\dfrac{20}{20} = \dfrac{100 \times 2}{100}$ <br> $\dfrac{25 + 200}{100 + 200} = \dfrac{225}{300} = 75\%$ | $\dfrac{40}{40} = \dfrac{100 \times 1}{100 \times 1}$ <br> $\dfrac{5}{20} = \dfrac{25 \times 2}{100 \times 2}$ <br> $\dfrac{100 + 50}{100 + 200} = \dfrac{150}{300} = 50\%$ |

Figure 5.3

percentage and then use weighting factors to create the final grade. Take a look at the information in Figure 5.3.

In Figure 5.3, the teacher intended that performance have double the weight of the paper-and-pencil test. Amanda did poorly on the test but achieved a perfect score on the performance assessment; Alan did very poorly on the performance but achieved a perfect score on the test. Examine the results by using three different alternatives for grade weighting. When the weighting factors were applied to the raw scores (alternative 1), both students received the same percentage mark to go in their grade. This clearly was not the teacher's intent; another approach is needed. By applying the weighting to the point values (alternative 2), the teacher ensured that performance was marked on a scale that was double that of the test scale. When the teacher used the common (percentage) scale (alternative 3), each aspect was marked using the same scale (100), and then the weighting factors were applied. Both alternative 2 and

SkyLight Training and Publishing Inc

## Grading Using a Common Scale

| Component | Learning Goal #1 | | | | | | | | | | | |
| --- | --- | --- | --- | --- | --- | --- | --- | --- | --- | --- | --- | --- |
| Assessment Method | Test | | | Performance | | | Test | | | | | |
| Weight | 1.5 | | | 4.0 | | | 2.0 | | | | | |
| Student | Mark out of 20 | Mark as a % | Weighted mark out of 150 | Mark out of 50 | Mark as a % | Weighted mark out of 400 | Mark out of 80 | Mark as a % | Weighted mark out of 200 | Raw score total 150 | Weighted score total 750 | Weighted score as a % |
| Julia | 20 | 100 | 150 | 20 | 40 | 160 | 60 | 75 | 150 | 100 | 460 | 61.3 |
| Derek | 10 | 50 | 75 | 50 | 100 | 400 | 40 | 50 | 100 | 100 | 575 | 76.7 |
| Brian | 20 | 100 | 150 | 0 | 0 | 0 | 80 | 100 | 200 | 100 | | |
| Brittany | 0 | 0 | 0 | 50 | 100 | 400 | 50 | 62.5 | 135 | 100 | | |

Figure 5.4

alternative 3 achieved the same result—Amanda's final mark was significantly higher than Alan's, which reflected the teacher's intent that performance have double the weight of the test. Although both alternatives achieve the intended weighting, the common scale approach is recommended because, over a one- or two-semester course, it is easier to use than continually balancing the total possible score, that is, weight the score with all the other assessments that count in the final grade.

Review the information in Figure 5.4. For the learning goal in this example, each assessment has a total score of the teacher's choosing, but the students' marks are recorded on a common scale (percentage) and the chosen weighting factors are then applied. In this example, Julia and Derek both receive the same raw score total, but when the raw scores are converted to a common scale, Derek's grade is significantly higher than Julia's. This reflects the fact that he achieved the maximum possible mark on the part of the assessment considered to be more important than the other two parts of the assessment taken together. This is what was intended—the teacher considered the performance to be more important than the two tests combined.

**The common scale approach is recommended.**

### Reflecting on . . . Weighting Grades

Consider the other two students in Figure 5.4. They both received the same raw scores as Julia and Derek. Calculate their weighted score totals and weighted scores as a percentage, then consider the following:

1. Do their final grades for this learning goal reflect the teacher's intent?

2. Taking into account the other guidelines in this book, what would you do with Brian and Brittany, that is, what grade would you include for learning goal #1 in your final grade calculation?

## The Issue of Variability of Scores

Technically, variability of scores on each assessment also needs to be taken into account, that is, a test with a range of scores from 40% to 80% has a different impact than a performance assessment for which the scores vary from 10% to 100%. It would be ideal if scores were equated through the use of standard scores before being weighted. For a detailed description of these procedures, see Thayer (1991).

Because there is enough in this guideline (let alone the other seven!) for teachers to consider without dealing with these highly technical issues, not much detail is provided here about standardizing scores. As Airasian suggested, "This is not a major problem with most classroom assessments, which generally are given in the same format to the same group of pupils, cover the topics taught, and are scored in the same way. Under these conditions the spread of scores on different assessments will usually be close enough so that adjustments need not be made" (1994, 318). The issue of variability of scores, however, is something that teachers need to be aware of, especially when class rank, scholarships, and awards are being determined.

> The issue of variability of scores is something that teachers need to be aware of.

## Reflecting on . . . Simple Averaging

Consider the situation shown in the chart.

|            | STEPHEN | MEGAN | HIGHEST GRADE IN SCHOOL |
|------------|---------|-------|-------------------------|
| English    | 96%     | 96%   | 96%                     |
| Chemistry  | 97%     | 96%   | 97%                     |
| Biology    | 96%     | 100%  | 100%                    |
| Physics    | 99%     | 99%   | 99%                     |
| Algebra    | 92%     | 92%   | 94%                     |
| Calculus   | 99%     | n/a   | 99%                     |
| Music      | n/a     | 89%   | 89%                     |

Each student stood first or had equal first grades in five subjects, but Stephen was first in calculus with 99% whereas Megan was first in music with 89%. If these grades are simply averaged, Stephen will be ranked first even though Megan had a slightly higher average on the five subjects that they each studied. Is this fair?

# Including Rubric Scores in Grades

Another aspect of number crunching that needs to be considered is how to include rubric scores in grades. One approach was suggested in Chapter 4; it is based on the ideas of Marzano and Kendall (1996, 151). They believed that teachers should not simply add numbers together over a semester or a year—what they call "the cumulative option"—but that, for each learning goal, teachers record scores in a variety of ways and then report a score for each learning goal. They acknowledged that this approach might not be acceptable in many school districts, so they suggested a "compromise solution" (158). The compromise solution includes the following:

1. Use well-informed teacher judgment to assign scores that represent levels of understanding and skill for specific standards (learning goals).

2. Have a written grading policy for each course that clearly describes how scores or standards are to be weighted.

3. Clearly communicate to students and parents which standards are included in the computation of grades and how standards are weighted. (157–158)

Review Figure 5.5, which depicts the use of Marzano and Kendall's approach. Assuming that their first suggestion (learning goals) is followed, a teacher's grade book might look like Figure 5.5. Decisions now have to be made on Marzano and Kendall's points 2 and 3.

## Scores Without Weighting

Assuming no weighting, there are two basic approaches that can be used. The first is total points; in Figure 5.5, Judy received scores on 30 assessments, for each of which the highest possible score was a 4, so the total possible points was 120. She received 86 points, which means she received 72%. This could be her final grade for the course.

The second approach is to consider frequency of scores. In this case, decisions are made about what would constitute an A, B, C, and so forth, for example, 80% of the scores at 3 or 4 with no scores below 2 could be an A, 50% scores at 3 or 4 with no scores below 2 could be a B, and so on. This approach could be applied to determine one overall grade or to determine a grade for each learning goal. If the latter approach is used, a frequency scale could be applied to determine the final overall grade.

> Teachers should not simply add numbers together over a semester or a year—but for each learning goal, record scores in a variety of ways and then report a score for each learning goal. (Marzana and Kendall, 1996)

# Judy's Scores in Grade 5 Social Studies
## Based on 4-point Rubric

| Learning Goal | Summative Assessment #1 | SA#2 | SA#3 | SA#4 | SA#5 | Total | Weight | Adjusted Total |
|---|---|---|---|---|---|---|---|---|
| 1 | 3 | 3 | 3 | 3 | 3 | 15 | 2 | 30 |
| 2 | 4 | 4 | 4 | 1 | 4 | 17 | 3 | 51 |
| 3 | 1 | 2 | 3 | 4 | 4 | 14 | 2 | 28 |
| 4 | 3 | 2 | 3 | 2 | 3 | 13 | 1 | 13 |
| 5 | 4 | 3 | 4 | 3 | 4 | 18 | 3 | 54 |
| 6 | 2 | 2 | 2 | 1 | 2 | 9 | 1 | 9 |
| Total | | | | | | 86/120 | | 185/240 |
| Percentage | | | | | | 71.7 | | 77.1 |

Figure 5.5

## Scores With Weighting

If the teacher's judgment leads to the conclusion that weighting is necessary, total weighted points may be used. In Figure 5.5, weights are provided and applied in the two right-hand columns. As a result, Judy received a weighted score of 185/240, giving her a final grade of 77%.

Another possible approach is to apply a simple conversion between rubric scores, percentage marks, and letters. For example:

| | | |
|---|---|---|
| 4 | 90%–100% | A |
| 3 | 80%–89% | B |
| 2 | 70%–79% | C |
| 1 | 60%–69% | D |
| 0 | less than 60% | F |

(If only percentage marks and grades are used, it would be necessary for teachers to assign an actual percentage for each assessment. This should be the top or near the top of the range for A to D, but for F, it is recommended that teachers exercise careful judgment. As indicated earlier, they need to be particularly careful about assigning very low percentages, especially zeros.)

An approach like this is probably the best one, especially for schools that have grading scales with relatively high cutoff scores, for example, an F is less than 70%.

The suggestions on how to convert rubric scores have been adapted from an activity in the Regional Educational Laboratories *Toolkit 98* (1998), which is based on a memo from Linda L. Elman, testing coordinator, to the teachers in her district in the state of Washington. In her conclusion, Elman says that each method, except for the frequency of scores method, "makes the method seem more scientific than it really is." Her final advice to teachers is

> once you, as a teacher arrive at a method of converting rubric scores to a scale that is comparable to other grades, the responsibility is on you to come up with a **defensible** system for weighting the pieces in the grade book to come up with a final grade for students. This part of the teaching process is part of the professional art of teaching. There is no single right way to do it; however whatever is done needs to reflect evidence of **students' level of mastery** of the targets of instruction. (Regional Educational Laboratory 1998, Handout A46, H3, p. 5)

For another approach to converting rubric scores to grades, see Linek (1991, 130–131).

## What's the Bottom Line?

How to crunch numbers?—Very carefully!

Consider

- the effect of various ways of calculating central tendency
- the effect of extreme marks
- how scores and/or learning goals should be weighted
- the effect of mark distribution
- how to include nontraditional scores (i.e., rubrics) in grades

The practical implication of Guideline 5 is that teachers need to exercise their professional judgment, not just use mechanical, numerical calculations when assigning grades. The real bottom line is, if Guideline 3 is consistently applied, Guideline 5 is almost not needed!

**There is no single right way to do it; however whatever is done needs to reflect evidence of students' level of mastery of the targets of instruction.** (Regional Educational Laboratory 1998, Handout A46, H3, p. 5)

# What's My Thinking Now?

Analyze Guideline 5 for grading (Crunch numbers carefully) by focusing on three questions:

Why use it?

Why not use it?

Points of uncertainty

After careful thought about these points, answer these two questions:

Would I use Guideline 5 now?

Do I agree or disagree with the guideline, or am I unsure at this time?

(See the following for one person's reflections on Guideline 5.)

# A Reflection on Guideline 5

*WHY USE IT?*

- median fairer than mean, allows for a stumble or two
- median reduces impact of low marks, especially zeros
- rewards improvement and progress
- weighting properly reflects importance of learning goal
- weighting properly reflects time spent on learning goal

*WHY NOT USE IT?*

- encourages students to not do every assignment
- mean always used by colleges and universities
- teachers don't have time for agreement on weighting
- medians too difficult to calculate
- often good reasons for a zero; should count

*POINTS OF UNCERTAINTY*

- totally new ideas so not sure students would understand
- what do grades mean when different procedures are used?
- what do zeros represent?
- how do you weight learning goals appropriately?
- parent reaction

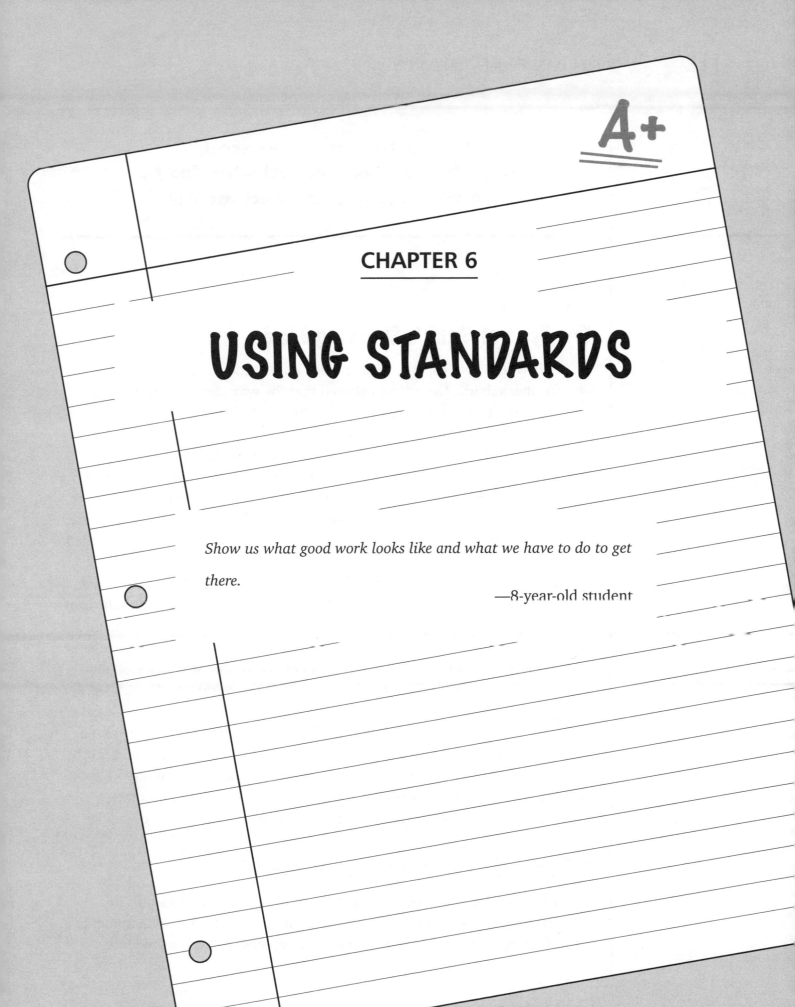

# CHAPTER 6

# USING STANDARDS

*Show us what good work looks like and what we have to do to get there.*

—8-year-old student

| GUIDELINE | Use criterion-referenced |
|:---:|:---:|
| **6** | **(i.e., absolute or preset) standards to distribute grades and marks.** |

**Students' grades should depend on their own achievement.**

## The Case of Sally's Shocking Grade

Sally was a very capable mathematics student in a small school in a high income suburb. The school believed that the way to ensure maximum student effort was to use a bell curve to distribute grades. Sally's junior math class was taught by Mrs. Jones, who was generally acknowledged to be an excellent teacher, and had only ten students in the class. Sally really enjoyed the class, believed she was learning effectively, and appeared to be achieving well as all her quiz, test, and performance scores were more than 80%. She was absolutely shocked when she received her first quarter report card, and her math grade was an F. Her parents immediately called the school to inquire why their daughter received a failing grade. They were informed that Sally's marks were the lowest in the class, thus she fell into the lowest category on the bell curve. Sally doubled her efforts in the second quarter, but she was in a class with nine absolutely brilliant math students, so at the end of the quarter, she was still in last place and received another F. Her parents could not accept this and arranged for Sally to transfer to a school with a semestered program. Sally enrolled in the same math course and continued to perform at the same level as she had in her previous school. In this school, Sally's 80%+ marks were the highest in the class, and she received a grade of A+! The difference in the two situations was not Sally's achievement, but rather the ability of her classmates. In both schools, Sally's grades were not fair or accurate representations of her mathematics achievement.

## What's the Purpose of the Guideline?

This guideline supports learning and encourages student success by ensuring that students' grades depend on their own achievement and do not depend on how that achievement compares with other students' achievements. Under this guideline, there is no artificial rationing of high (or low) grades as there is when relative standards (norm-referencing or the bell curve) are used to distribute grades.

# What Are the Key Elements of the Guideline?

Everybody believes in standards, preferably high standards. But often it is not clear what is meant by standards. The use of standards always involves comparison and judgment because we are trying to answer the questions "how good is it?" or "how good is good enough?"

## Developing Standards: Five Methods

One might suggest that these questions are impossible to answer, but here are five ways of approaching standards and standard setting:

1. Develop a norm.
2. Develop a criterion.
3. Use tacit knowledge.
4. Describe verbally.
5. Use key examples.

This five-fold classification is helpful because it shows a variety of standards or standard-setting approaches. Let us review each method in more detail.

### Standard Based on a Norm

A *norm* is usually a number (often a mean) that is used as a standard against which performance is measured or compared (e.g., IQ test scores). Norms always compare one's performance with performances of others and are used appropriately in competitions when ranking is necessary. The concept of norms is expressed most clearly in the bell curve or so-called "normal distribution." This concept holds that there will be an equal number of high and low performers and that, on any performance, a population will be spread as shown in Figure 6.1.

### Standard Based on a Criterion

A *criterion* is a reference point, often a number, against which performance is measured, for example, words per minute in keyboarding. Criterion-referenced standards also compare, but the comparison is with a

**Often it is not clear what is meant by standards.**

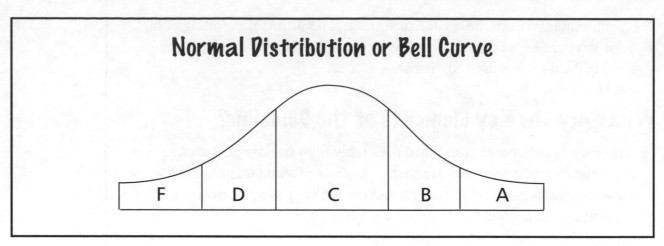

Figure 6.1

**In the real world, standards often involve combining several approaches.**

performance level, not the performance of others. For example, the world-class standard for the 100 meters is 10 seconds. Any runner near this time is a world-class sprinter, but we would not expect a 12-year-old runner to perform at this level. We can, however, use the world-class time as a basis for criterion-referenced standards at various age groups.

### Standard Based on Tacit Knowledge

Tacit knowledge belongs to the expert or connoisseur. These standards may begin as criterion-referenced standards but, in their highest form, reside only in the head of the expert. This level of knowledge comes only as a result of many years of study and/or practice. An example of this standard is Olympic skating scores.

### Standard Based on Verbal Description

Verbal description involves statements that make a standard explicit, public, and accessible, so that the standard is known and can be met and challenged, for example, by prior learning assessment.

### Standard Based on Key Examples

Key examples of performance or behavior can be shown in various formats, including visual or text form, to help people recognize the standard when they see it. Exemplars are not standards but rather represent standards, for example, videotaped performances of oral presentations.

### Standard Based on Combinations of Methods

It is important to note that, in the real world, standards often involve combining several of these approaches. In figure skating, criteria are applied by experts using their tacit knowledge to arrive at a score on technical merit and artistic impression for each performance; however, to arrive at the final result for the competition, each skater's scores are compared with all the other skaters' scores to rank them (ordinals) and to determine the final placing for each skater for that performance. It is also worth noting that the expert's tacit knowledge has been developed from verbal descriptions of the criteria and also from many hours of study of key examples, either in live performances or on video.

## Setting Standards for the Classroom

The question that has to be addressed is how should standards be established in and for the classroom?

### Using Self-Referencing

One standard that has a place is self-referencing—how is Sally doing today compared with how she did yesterday? How is she doing this month compared to last month? Last year? But even in this use of standards, decisions are made about what type of standard to use—is Sally compared with others? with performance criteria? based on expert knowledge, descriptions and/or exemplars?

### Using Norm Referencing

Traditionally, the bell curve has been used to assign marks and grades, especially at the college level. This approach has many problems, which are eloquently summarized by both Guskey and Bellanca:

> Grading on a curve makes learning a highly competitive activity in which students compete against one another for the few scarce rewards (high grades) distributed by the teacher. Under these conditions, students readily see that helping others become successful threatens their own chances for success. As a result, learning becomes a game of winners and losers; and because the number of rewards is kept arbitrarily small, most students are forced to be losers. (Guskey 1996, 18–19)

> Grades, especially those based on the competitive curve, create fearsome anxieties for students . . . as well as for teachers. In our highly individualistic society, the grading curve exacerbates the most negative aspects of competition. Because the grading curve brands winners and losers, it works against the goal of successful learning for all students. . . . For every student who wins with an A, there is one who loses with a B, C or F. As the top scorers become more enamored

**Because the grading curve brands winners and losers, it works against the goal of successful learning for all students.** (Bellanca 1992, 299)

of their successes in school, one by one, the bottom dwellers give up and go elsewhere. (Bellanca 1992, 299)

This idea was expressed more simply by Glasser when he said "no student grade should ever depend on what other students do" (1990, 108).

In addition to this philosophical argument, there are also technical reasons why the use of the bell curve is inappropriate. In order to establish a normal distribution, the sample size must be large (at least several hundred, preferably thousands). It is simply wrong to grade on the curve if the population size is small. To be technically correct, one could use the curve at the classroom level, but only for very large classes, for example, all freshman English students in a very large high school or college. Even in this situation, philosophical (and practical) considerations should lead teachers away from the bell curve. Consider this: The class whose marks/grades are curved may be the best—or worst—the school has ever had. If it is the best, many students receive much lower grades than they really deserve; if it is the worst, many students receive much higher grades than they really deserve.

This unappealing situation is described by Pratt (1980, 253). He described the distributions of grades for two consecutive presentations of the same course by the same instructor. The first semester class was very weak, achieving final scores of 0% to 55%; the second semester class was much stronger, achieving final scores of 40% to 100%. The instructor followed his usual practice of bell curving the results and giving students final letter grades of A to F. In this somewhat extreme example, students who received an F in the second semester would have received an A with the same score in the first semester!

It is clear from this example that grading on a curve tells very little about what students know or are able to do. Grades are meant to be vehicles of clear communication—grading on the curve does not meet this standard because it often provides grades that are almost meaningless as measures of achievement.

An argument often made for the use of norm referencing in classroom grades is that it maintains standards. As noted earlier, this is not always the case—if you have a very weak class, students who do not deserve A's will get them if the bell curve is used. An extreme example of this occurred in California immediately after World War II. Many returning servicemen (and they were almost all men!) enrolled in college as a result

> **There are technical reasons why the use of the bell curve is inappropriate.**

of the GI bill; at this time, virtually all colleges used the bell curve. Aware of this, some men got their wives to enroll in the same courses as they did. Because the wives did no work and therefore got the Fs on the curve, the husbands were guaranteed higher grades!

As Rick Stiggins said in a workshop presentation in Toronto in May, 1992, "There is no pedagogical, psychological, or scientific reason to assume in advance that achievement will be distributed in any way—whether normally or skewed in some direction—before instruction begins." Therefore, norm referencing or the bell curve are not appropriate at the classroom level. He went on to say, "Standards ought to be reflected, not in some . . . assumption of what the distribution of grades should be, but in clear, rigorous targets for students. Grading should be based on clear, high quality assessment of students' achievement with respect to that target."

## Using Criterion Referencing

If norm referencing does not work, then we must use criterion-referenced standards. At times, these standards involve numbers, but more often they are verbal descriptions of various levels of performance (rubrics) developed from the tacit knowledge of experts (teachers, in collaboration with their students) supported by key examples of quality products, performances, or behaviors (e.g., see Chapter 4, Figure 4.5).

The more people involved in the discussions and decisions on these criterion-referenced standards, the better. Determining the standards, whether for Grade 1 visual arts, senior mathematics, or college biology, is not an easy task. Equally vital is that the criterion-referenced standards have credibility with the students, teachers, parents, and the community where they are used. Spady suggested the "criteria need to be focused on the true culminating outcomes of significance for our students—not on all the daily details and work tasks" (1991, 44). A generic rather than a task-specific approach may help, but it is extremely difficult—if not impossible—to achieve complete agreement on what quality is. Decisions do have to be made, and the standards chosen will have much greater credibility if they are public, and if the process by which they were determined is open and accessible. This does not mean that there needs to be a public standard-setting process for each assessment used, but teachers need to be able to align the standards they are using with publicly available standards.

**It is extremely difficult—if not impossible—to achieve complete agreement on what quality is. Standards chosen will have much greater credibility if they are public.**

## Reflecting on . . . Sample Scenarios

Take a minute to consider these situations:

1. What do you think would happen in your school if you did an outstanding job, all the students in your class were highly motivated and did an outstanding job, and all the students received grades of 90% or higher?

2. What do you think would happen in your school if you did a good job, most of the students in your class were unmotivated and did a poor job, and almost all the students received failing grades?

If the school's objective for grades is to support learning and encourage success, situation #1 needs to be celebrated. But situation #2 needs to be carefully examined, and program decisions need to be made to try to ensure that it does not happen again.

Far too often, however, neither situation would be allowed. In situation 1, administrators frequently lower student grades or at least severely question the teacher. As Juarez pointed out "normative grading forces the teacher into the absurd 'Catch 22' position of not being viewed as successful unless a percentage of his or her students are unsuccessful" (1990, 37). In situation 2, student grades would probably be raised and the teacher's competence doubted.

Neither of these administrative decisions is acceptable. If all students perform at a high—or at a low—level, then they should receive the appropriate marks and grades. There should be no artificial rationing of high or low marks or grades. This is particularly important in the so-called subjective subjects, such as English and history; students must be able to receive 100% in these subjects in the same way as students get 100% in the so-called objective subjects, such as mathematics and physics. Marks or grades of 100% do "not indicate perfection, but rather that the student has achieved all 'objectives' at the highest standard identified" (Pratt 1980, 257).

It is also critical that there be no grade rationing in different years in school or college. It appears that many high school teachers, and particularly first year college teachers, claim they have high standards because their class averages are low, many students fail, and few students receive A's. This view is examined thoughtfully, and somewhat humorously, by Bonstingl (1992) in a chapter titled "The Bell Curve Meets Kaizen" (*kaizen* means continuous improvement). He posed this question—"Why

> There should be no artificial rationing of high or low marks or grades.

does it seem the farther we get from first grade, the less likely we are to view education's central purpose as nurturing people's innate potential through the development of patterns of success, and the more likely we are to view education as a judgmental, gatekeeping function?" (2–3)

Marks and grades must reflect actual student performance based on publicly available criterion-referenced standards, not artificially determined distributions. Cereal and car makers strive to produce 100% of their products with a grade of A—educators must strive for this as well, and not be satisfied with class averages of about 70%, which is often the case. Teachers must be careful that they do not have a bell curve lurking in the backs of their minds; they must be prepared to give students the grade they deserve based on comparison with absolute (criterion-referenced), not relative (norm-referenced), standards.

## What's the Bottom Line?

What standards should be used?—Criterion-referenced (or absolute) standards that are public, based on expert knowledge, clearly stated in words or numbers, and supported by exemplars or models.

> **Marks and grades must reflect actual student performance based on publicly available criterion-referenced standards.**

# What's My Thinking Now?

Analyze Guideline 6 for grading (Use criterion-referenced [i.e., absolute or preset] standards to distribute grades and marks) by focusing on three questions:

Why use it?

Why not use it?

Points of uncertainty

After careful thought about these points, answer these two questions:

Would I use Guideline 6 now?

Do I agree or disagree with the guideline, or am I unsure at this time?

(See the following for one person's reflections on Guideline 6.)

# A Reflection on Guideline 6

## WHY USE IT?

- clear to all what the standards are
- all learners may be successful
- emphasizes self-assessment and growth, not competition
- makes marking/grading more objective, consistent
- contributes to improved quality of work

## WHY NOT USE IT?

- time consuming to develop criteria, rubrics, etc.
- who says what quality is?
- doesn't teach competitiveness students need in "real" world
- standards may be set too high or too low
- need for flexibility, creativity

## POINTS OF UNCERTAINTY

- differences between teachers and schools on what is quality
- what do parents and the next level of educators expect?
- subject requirements vary, some more subjective than others
- variation in ability between and within classes
- can all students get As?

**CHAPTER 7**

# DEVELOPING ASSESSMENT QUALITY AND KEEPING RECORDS

*The grades awarded will only be as good as the formal assessment information on which they are based. The meaningfulness of grades depends on the meaningfulness of the assessments on which they are based. . . . Irrelevant, invalid evidence about pupil achievement will produce irrelevant, invalid grades.*

—Airasian (1994, 305)

# Use quality assessments and properly record evidence of achievement.

## The Case of Brian's Boosted Grade

Brian was a very good student in academic subjects. He was a high-quality critical thinker with a good memory and writing skills. He did not do well in technical or vocational subjects because, as he was all thumbs, he did not enjoy these courses and made little effort to complete quality products. His high school required all freshmen to take one technical or vocational course. Brian chose carpentry because his best friends had chosen it.

Brian's school had a very traditional approach to assessment, with middle and end of semester paper and pencil exams. Grades in the carpentry course were based partly on the students' products and partly on the written exams. Brian received failing marks on each of the required products, but he received perfect marks on the exams, which asked students to do such things as list safety procedures and describe how to build a bird house. At the middle and end of the semester, the carpentry teacher assigned a mark for attitude and participation. Knowing how to play the game and appearing to be interested and involved, Brian received a very high mark in this category. His final grade was 74%, which came from the following mark breakdown:

| PRODUCTS (40%) | | | | ATTITUDE/PARTICIPATION (20%) | | EXAMS (40%) | |
|---|---|---|---|---|---|---|---|
| Possible score: | 30 | 70 | 40 | 60 | 20 | 20 | 100 | 100 |
| Brian's score: | 11 | 24 | 10 | 27 | 20 | 20 | 100 | 100 |
| Mean Score: | 36% | | | | 100% | | 100% | |

Brian's teacher neither followed quality assessment principles nor recorded evidence throughout the semester. Brian received an inflated grade—assuming that the main learning goal was the demonstration of carpentry skills.

# What's the Purpose of the Guideline?

This guideline supports learning and encourages student success by ensuring that each student's grade comes from quality assessments, the results of which have been recorded accurately and in a timely manner. The issue here is that all involved understand the critical dimensions of quality assessment. The other component requires teachers to keep accurate records and not rely on memory.

# What Are the Key Elements of the Guideline?

## Dimensions of Quality Assessment

Marks and grades are meaningful when—and only when—they are based on quality assessment. Thus, it is essential that teachers know, understand, and apply quality standards when they plan and implement assessment in their classrooms. According to Stiggins (1997, 14–16), these quality standards include:

> Targets—appropriate and clear
>
> Purpose—clear
>
> Matching—method to target and purpose
>
> Sample—appropriate for the learning domain
>
> Interference—all sources controlled

Let us briefly review each standard.

### Setting Targets

The importance of clear and appropriate targets cannot be overstated. If we do not know where we want to go, then we do not need a map to get there; but if we want to know how to get from point A to point B, we need a map. In the classroom, the "map" is provided by the learning goals that have been prescribed or established for each grade or course. In most courses, targets are

- knowledge—what students are to know
- application of knowledge (reasoning and skills)—what students are able to do
- values/attitudes—what students are like, that is, how they behave

**Marks and grades are meaningful when—and only when—they are based on quality assessment.**

In order to meet the standard in this guideline, teachers—and students—must understand what is being assessed and what constitutes quality performance. Suggestions about how this standard can be met are found in Chapters 4 and 8.

## Stating Purpose

Clear purpose comes from understanding why the assessment is being conducted and what use will be made of the assessment results by the many potential users—at the classroom level (students, teachers, and parents), at the instructional support level (remedial teachers, school building administrators, central office support personnel), and at the policy level (district administrators, school board trustees, state/provincial department personnel). All these users have different needs, but as Stiggins said, "There is no single assessment capable of meeting all these different needs. Thus, the developer of any assessment must start with a clear sense of whose needs the assessment will meet" (1997, 16). At the classroom level, which is the focus of this book, this standard means that the teacher needs a very clear understanding of purpose, that is, whether for diagnosis or for formative or summative assessment, and whether and how the results will be included in student grades. Detailed consideration of these issues is found in Chapter 2.

## Matching Method With Target

Matching method with target requires that the assessor choose a method of assessment that is capable of providing the needed information. If knowledge of vocabulary in French is the target, then a selected response test is an appropriate choice; but if the target is the student's ability to speak French, then a performance assessment is needed. Meeting this standard is made easier by the fact that there are many different assessment methods available for use. They may be classified as paper and pencil tests, performance assessment, and personal communication (see Figure Intro.3). Matching assessments with targets, which may be part or all of specified learning goals, requires that teachers know and understand targets and learning goals, know and understand various methods of assessment, and put the methods and targets/learning goals together.

## Reflecting on . . . Assessment Methodology

Decide which assessment methods match with which learning goals in the following chart.

> **The developer of any assessment must start with a clear sense of whose needs the assessment will meet.** (Stiggins 1997, 16)

| Assessment Methods  Types of Learning Goals | Paper and Pencil Tests *(selected response)* | Performance Assessment *(constructed response, product, performance, process)* | Personal Communications *(conversation, observation)* |
|---|---|---|---|
| Knowledge | | | |
| Application of Knowledge *(Skills, Reasoning, Products)* | | | |
| Values/Attitudes *(Affect/Behavior)* | | | |

**The emphasis needs to be put on "knowledge in use" not "knowledge about."**

Place a check mark (√) in boxes where there is a match and a cross (x) in those boxes where there is no match. Use an asterisk (*) to indicate the best matches for knowledge and application of knowledge. You may want to add a few words to explain your understanding of appropriate matches.

When you have completed this exercise, compare your responses with the choices shown in Figure 7.1.

Figure 7.1 may serve as a guide for teachers. Matching method with target requires choices that will give an accurate picture of student achievement, while taking into account the human, material, and time resources available in the classroom.

Matching also requires that assessments do what they are intended to do in another way. Figure 7.2 suggests that reasoning questions can tap five types of thinking skills, ranging from recall to evaluation. If test or exam questions are aimed at comparison, inference, analysis, and/or evaluation and are really matched to these skills, then the questions must present situations that are new to students, so that they can apply their knowledge. The emphasis needs to be put on "knowledge in use" not "knowledge about." Teachers often think that they ask students higher-level thinking skill questions, but if, for example, a comparison of two battles has been taught in class, a question asking students to compare the two battles is a recall question.

# Matching Assessment and Learning Goals

| Assessment Methods<br><br>Types of Learning Goals | Paper-and-Pencil Tests *(selected response)* | Performance Assessment *(constructed response, product, performance, process)* | Personal Communications *(conversation, observation)* |
|---|---|---|---|
| Knowledge | * ✔ | ✔ | ✔ |
| Application of Knowledge *(Skills, Reasoning, Products)* | X | * ✔ | ✔ |
| Values/Attitudes *(Affect/Behavior)* | ✔ | ✔ | ✔ |

Figure 7.1

# Test Specification Chart

| Type of Thinking \ Content | Concept #1 | Concept #2 | Concept #3 | Concept #4 | Total |
|---|---|---|---|---|---|
| Recall | 2 (5)* | 2 (5) | 2 (5) | 2 (5) | 8 (20) |
| Comparison | 1 (5) | | 1 (5) | | 2 (10) |
| Inference | | 1 (10) | | 1 (10) | 2 (20) |
| Analysis | | 1 (10) | 1 (10) | | 2 (20) |
| Evaluation | 1 (15) | | | 1 (15) | 2 (30) |

*The first figure is the number of items; (   ) is the percentage value of the test.

Figure 7.2

SkyLight Training and Publishing Inc

## Selecting Samples

Sample selection is necessary because, in all assessment situations, only part of the learning domain can be chosen and because there are practical time and length considerations. Returning to the French example introduced on page 126—in a vocabulary test, a representative sample of the words a student is supposed to know is used, whereas, in a speaking ability performance, students speak long enough for an accurate assessment of their ability to be made.

Careful planning is the key to sample selection for all assessment methods. All require that teachers think carefully about what will be included so that valid inferences can be made about student achievement. For example, for paper-and-pencil tests, teachers may use some form of test specification chart in which they check that each thinking skill and all the content is sampled. See Figure 7.2 on page 128. Planning of this type should lead to teachers being able to draw confident conclusions about student achievement.

## Controlling Interference

Interference or distortion from all sources must be controlled as much as possible in all assessment situations. Stiggins said teachers need to "design, develop, and use assessments in ways that permit us to control for all sources of bias and distortion that can cause our results to misrepresent real student achievement" (1997, 16). How often have we heard teachers say things like "Dexter's grade in (some subject) doesn't represent what he knows and can do because he doesn't test well"? If Stiggins' advice is followed, the teacher will adjust for Dexter's test problems, for example, by providing him with an alternative method or more time to demonstrate his real achievement.

Bias or distortion can occur in a number of circumstances:

1. With all methods of assessments for all students (e.g., physical conditions—noise, lighting, seating; motivation; assessment anxiety; poorly worded directions or questions).

2. With all methods of assessments for some students (e.g., emotional or physical health; reading/language ability; testwiseness).

3. With specific methods of assessment (e.g., multiple choice—more than one correct response; performance assessment, including essay questions—criteria inappropriate or lacking).

> Interference or distortion from all sources must be controlled as much as possible in all assessment situations.

(Further detail on sources of bias can be found in Stiggins and Knight, 1997, 56.)

The most common source of distortion in the assessment of student achievement is time—or the lack of it—because most assessments are time limited. Students who know and can achieve the learning goal(s), but who work slowly and need a lot of time to demonstrate their achievement, have their achievement misrepresented when they are forced to rush their work or when they are unable to complete an assessment activity. There are some skills that do need to be demonstrated in a timed manner, for example, words per minute in keyboarding, but for most other knowledge and skills, the critical dimension is—or should be—quality, not speed.

Many students who achieve at high levels need considerable time to reflect and analyze before they are able to produce quality work. Other students are simply methodical and slow in their approach, and some simply write slowly. Teachers need to take these personal differences into account and be flexible with time limits. This problem is usually most obvious in tests and exams. Teachers may help students, for example, by always testing in the period before a break and by providing some flex-time in examination schedules.

The complexity of this issue and the problem of trying to give students challenging tasks on exams was described beautifully by Manon:

> . . . trying to crowd together several important tasks into one fretful hour makes no sense at all. . . . That our students ever complete a finished product on a timed mathematics test is indeed quite remarkable. Asking them to do their best work under such constraints is nether productive nor fair. Even the most accomplished of mathematicians would not wait till an hour before publication to begin work on *someone else's* [italics in original] hard problem. (1995, 140)

In the same article, Manon acknowledged that a difficult question he had put on an exam "should rightly have been posed as an extended exploration" (139). He realized that "the students had not been given adequate time or resources to complete the problem" and that "discovery on demand is a highly risky business" (140).

If teachers know that student marks and grades are not a true reflection of their achievement, it is almost certainly because one or more of the quality standards has not been maintained. In such situations, teachers must remember that grading is (or should be) an exercise in professional judgment, not just a mechanical, numerical exercise.

# Keeping Records

The second part of Guideline 7 requires teachers to keep careful and timely records of student achievement. The key point here is that records must be recorded somewhere—on paper or on a computer—not just held in a teacher's head.

There are, of course, myriad ways for teachers to keep appropriate records. Records need to be as individualized as possible, so the best approach is to have a separate page for each student (e.g., Figure 7.3). This is manageable when teachers have a home room or core group, but it is very difficult for teachers in a rotary system, who will probably see 100 to 200 students each day. In these situations, teachers need to adapt the individual student sheets or forms to whole class use. One such sheet is shown in Figure 7.4. This sheet can accommodate many students, and records can be kept for a number of learning goals. As shown in Figure 7.3, teachers may use a variety of symbols to identify student achievement (rubric scores, marks, etc.). It is important that this sheet is organized by learning goals, not methods of assessment. This desirable approach was discussed in Chapter 1 see in particular, Figure 4.4.

Figure 7.5 summarizes the variety of assessment methods available and suggests a variety of recording approaches. Use of these assessment methods and recording approaches will provide teachers with a rich variety of achievement information—a student profile—on which to base grading decisions. Terwilliger (1989) suggested that all data collected for the purpose of judging student achievement should be expressed in quantitative form, but this is probably necessary only for summative assessments and in the later years of high school and in college. Depending on grade level and subject, teachers decide which of the recording approaches are practical and appropriate for them and their students.

**Records need to be as individual as possible.**

# Student Achievement
### *Summary for Grading/Reporting Purposes*

Program Area(s)/Subject(s): _____

Student: _____ Class: _____

| SCORING (e.g., one of:)<br>*Levels:* 4 (high) – 1 (poor)<br>*Marks:* out of "x" or %<br>*Scale:* E, S, N (Exceptional, Standard, Needs Improvement)<br>*Completion:* ✔ or x | Assessment Task | | | | | | | | | Highest Most Consistent Level of Achievement | |
|---|---|---|---|---|---|---|---|---|---|---|---|
| **Strands/Outcomes** | | | | | | | | | | | **Anecdotal Comments** |
| | | | | | | | | | | | |
| | | | | | | | | | | | |
| | | | | | | | | | | | |
| | | | | | | | | | | | |
| | | | | | | | | | | | |
| | | | | | | | | | | | |
| | | | | | | | | | | | |
| | | | | | | | | | | | |
| | | | | | | | | | | | |

A variety of assessment strategies would be used to gather data for this summary. These strategies would identify the specific learning outcome(s) being assessed.

Adapted by permission from a chart developed by Damian Cooper, Halton District Board of Education, Ontario.

Figure 7.3

SkyLight Training and Publishing Inc

## Class List for _____

Student achievement in the classroom setting can be "tracked" if proper records are kept. Use ✓ or **x** (done, not done), rubric scores, marks, or any suitable scoring scale to record student achievement.

| Learning Goals | Student Names | | | | | | | | | | | | | | | | | | | | | | | | | | | | | | |
|---|---|---|---|---|---|---|---|---|---|---|---|---|---|---|---|---|---|---|---|---|---|---|---|---|---|---|---|---|---|---|---|
| | | | | | | | | | | | | | | | | | | | | | | | | | | | | | | | | |
| | | | | | | | | | | | | | | | | | | | | | | | | | | | | | | | | |
| | | | | | | | | | | | | | | | | | | | | | | | | | | | | | | | | |
| | | | | | | | | | | | | | | | | | | | | | | | | | | | | | | | | |
| | | | | | | | | | | | | | | | | | | | | | | | | | | | | | | | | |
| | | | | | | | | | | | | | | | | | | | | | | | | | | | | | | | | |
| | | | | | | | | | | | | | | | | | | | | | | | | | | | | | | | | |
| | | | | | | | | | | | | | | | | | | | | | | | | | | | | | | | | |

Adapted from material developed for the Scarborough Board of Education, Ontario, Canada.

Figure 7.4

## Assessment Methods

| Assessment Method | | Recording Approaches |
|---|---|---|
| Personal Communication | Observation Conversation | ✓ or **x** (done or not done) <br> Rubric Score <br> Letter or Number Mark (x/10, %, A, B) |
| Performance Assessment | Product Performance Process | Symbol (G - good; S - satisfactory, NI - needs improvement) <br> Anecdotal Comment |
| Paper-and-Pencil Tests | Constructed Response Selected Response | Score: Number or Proportion Correct |

Figure 7.5

# What's the Bottom Line?

Quality assessment and accurate written or electronic record keeping are essential if grades are to reflect real student achievement. There are practical implications of Guideline 7:

- Teachers need to be aware of and apply the five standards of quality assessment.

- Teachers need to keep records on paper or on the computer—not in their heads.

# What's My Thinking Now?

Analyze Guideline 7 for grading (Use quality assessments and properly record evidence of achievement) by focusing on three questions:

Why use it?

Why not use it?

Points of uncertainty

After careful thought about these points, answer these two questions:

Would I use Guideline 7 now?

Do I agree or disagree with the guideline, or am I unsure at this time?

(See the following for one person's reflections on Guideline 7.)

# A Reflection on Guideline 7

## WHY USE IT?

- professional responsibility
- inspires greater confidence from students, parents
- provides real measure of achievement
- fair to learners
- ensures varied and appropriate assessment

## WHY NOT USE IT?

- amount of paper needed to record everything
- amount of time needed to record everything
- time needed to ensure quality is too great
- lack of available quality assessments
- tracking learning goals much more difficult than recording marks

## POINTS OF UNCERTAINTY

- subjective nature of some assessments
- who determines validity and reliability?
- level of assessment literacy
- who determines quality?
- political agenda

SkyLight Training and Publishing Inc

# CHAPTER 8

# COMMUNICATING WITH STUDENTS ABOUT GRADES

*We must constantly remind ourselves that the ultimate purpose of education is to have students become self-evaluating. If students graduate from our schools still dependent on others to tell them when they are adequate, good, or excellent, then we have missed the whole point of what education is about.*

— Costa and Kallick (1992, 280)

GUIDELINE

8

# Discuss assessment, including grading, with students at the beginning of instruction.

**The issue here is that students did not know what was included in grade calculations for their class.**

## The Case of Huang's Lunchtime Surprise

It was early November, fall sports had just finished, and it was almost time for midsemester exams and reports. The junior boys' volleyball team was having a pizza lunch to celebrate their season—they had won only one game, but most of the team were first-year players and had greatly improved over the course of the season. As well as their skill development and their improved understanding of game strategy, they had also developed a very strong team spirit. Thus, the time and effort they put in was fun and worthwhile, even if their team record did not suggest a successful season. About fifteen minutes into the luncheon, the coach noted that Huang, their best defensive player, and one who had never missed a practice or a game, was absent. He asked about this and was told that Huang and several other students had stayed behind in English class to discuss their grades with Ms. Hector. A few minutes later, Huang arrived at the luncheon; it was obvious that he was upset as he joined in the celebration in a very half-hearted manner.

At the end of the luncheon, the coach asked Huang to stay and share with him why he was upset. Huang explained that his first quarter English grade, which would be a significant portion of his final grade, was much lower than he expected. Ms. Hector had included a number of scores that Huang and other students thought were not going to be included. Most of these were for what they thought were practice activities in the first three weeks of classes.

Whether or not these scores should have been included relates to other grading guidelines (see Chapters 2 and 3). The issue here is that Huang and other students did not know what was included in grade calculations for their English class. This was in contrast to the assessment approach used on the volleyball team. For the team, the coach had stressed that the measure of the season would not be their won/lost record but their growth in skills and strategy and their enjoyment of practices, games, and the team experience. Throughout the season, he gave feedback to individuals and the team on their progress and growth in these areas; their league matches and the final luncheon were the summative assessment!

# What's the Purpose of the Guideline?

This guideline requires that the assessment practices, including how grades will be determined, are discussed with and are known to students from the beginning of instruction in each class. When students know how they will be assessed, and especially when they have been involved in assessment decisions, the likelihood of student success is increased greatly.

# What Are the Key Elements of the Guideline?

From nursery school to graduate school, teachers strive, or should strive, for student growth and progress on stated learning goals. Application of this guideline is obviously very different at different ages. What is important is the principle that students will be involved—student-centered assessment, as Rick Stiggins calls it—and know how and why they are being assessed.

## Student Involvement in Assessment

Several factors are involved in this discussion of student involvement and assessment, as follows:

- the balance between student involvement and teacher decision making

- age appropriateness

- the amount of detail provided students about assessment

- what is meant by the beginning of instruction

### Student Involvement and Teacher Decision Making

Giving students real opportunities for meaningful input into decisions about the how and what of classroom assessment, including grading, does not mean that students take over the teacher's professional responsibility to decide about assessment. There are several decisions that can be discussed with students. One is how they will demonstrate their competence on the learning goals of a course. Armstrong (1994, 125) provided

> **When students know how they will be assessed, and especially when they have been involved in assessment decisions, the likelihood of student success is increased greatly.**

an example of this by designing a form for students to indicate the type of performance assessment they would like to use to show their ability. Armstrong provided a list of possible assessment activities from which students might choose, but students also were allowed to add their own suggestions to the list. Teachers could adapt this form to match the learning goals in their schools and provide a customized form for each main learning goal in each course.

A second type of decision in which students could be involved concerns how to mark or score each assessment.

> Teachers can set criteria for their students. Teachers can set criteria with their students. Students can set or negotiate their own criteria. [There are] many ways to involve students in setting criteria. . . . when students take part in developing criteria, they are much more likely to understand what is expected of them, "buy in," and then accomplish the task successfully. (Gregory, Cameron, and Davies 1997, 7)

Criteria development may involve a marking scheme, a checklist, or a fully developed rubric.

The rubric shown in Figure 8.1 was developed by Grade 9 students in collaboration with their teachers. The students brainstormed the characteristics of an oral presentation; the teachers provided the categories; the students classified the characteristics; and then, the teachers provided the measurement scale (which is not very good!). The total class time to develop this rubric was about 25 minutes. Time well spent, both in principle and in practice, because in the class in which it was first used, 22 of 23 students performed in the top half of the scale. Even more significant was that all 23 students said they enjoyed doing the oral presentation, when previously it had been something that they hated doing.

A third example of decision making that involves students in their own assessment can be found in Sperling (1993). She described how the students in Gail Hughes' Grade 4 classroom in Ann Arbor, Michigan, developed their understanding of what good writing is by scoring writing samples and then developing a written list of criteria. Students were helped in this with examples of scored writing samples from their teacher. Sperling called this "collaborative assessment," and, although she acknowledged that it required a great deal of work by teachers, she concluded that "the results far outweigh the effort. Because criteria are

**Because criteria are clearly spelled out, students can take the responsibility to evaluate their own work.** (Sperling 1993, 75)

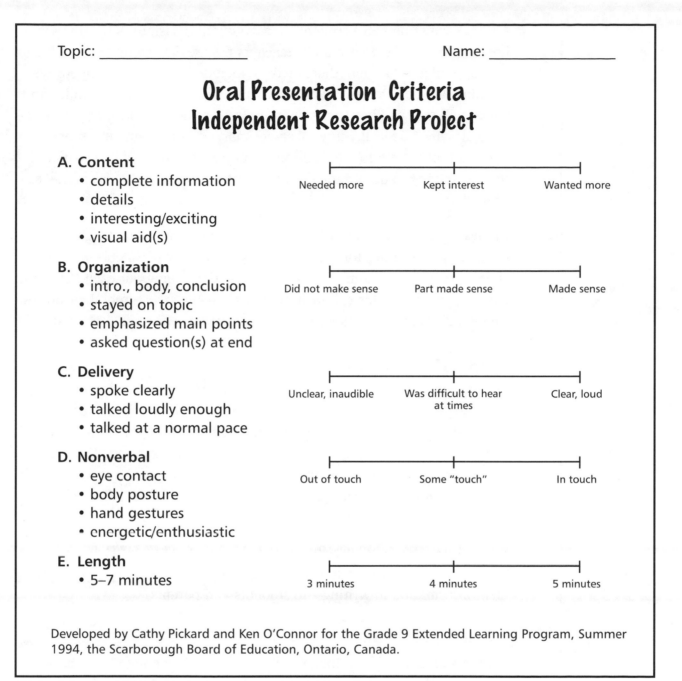

Topic: _____  Name: _____

# Oral Presentation Criteria
# Independent Research Project

**A. Content**
- complete information
- details
- interesting/exciting
- visual aid(s)

Needed more — Kept interest — Wanted more

**B. Organization**
- intro., body, conclusion
- stayed on topic
- emphasized main points
- asked question(s) at end

Did not make sense — Part made sense — Made sense

**C. Delivery**
- spoke clearly
- talked loudly enough
- talked at a normal pace

Unclear, inaudible — Was difficult to hear at times — Clear, loud

**D. Nonverbal**
- eye contact
- body posture
- hand gestures
- energetic/enthusiastic

Out of touch — Some "touch" — In touch

**E. Length**
- 5–7 minutes

3 minutes — 4 minutes — 5 minutes

Developed by Cathy Pickard and Ken O'Connor for the Grade 9 Extended Learning Program, Summer 1994, the Scarborough Board of Education, Ontario, Canada.

Figure 8.1

clearly spelled out, students can take the responsibility to evaluate their own work. They compare their self-assessment with the teacher's assessment, set goals for future work, and initiate corrective action to improve their own work" (1993, 75). Kohn said this involvement in determining criteria and then judging their work using these criteria "achieves several things at once: it gives students more control of their education, it makes evaluation feel less punitive, and it provides an important learning experience in itself" (1993a, 13).

A fourth way to involve students in assessment decisions is by discussing how grades will be determined. Teachers may review some of the difficult issues, such as what ingredients will be included (e.g., how cooperative learning will be assessed), which activities will be marked for grades and which will not, and how performance over a semester, term, or year will be dealt with, especially if work shows marked improvement. Students may also contribute to the decision about how grades will be calculated, that is, helping to determine the weighting factors and the use of means or medians.

In these four types of decisions, it is important to note that teachers provide opportunities for students to discuss how assessments will be chosen, scored, and combined, but that the decision about each issue rests with the teachers. This is how it needs to be—teachers apply their professional judgment and balance student suggestions with policy regulations.

**The decision about each issue rests with the teachers.**

## Age Appropriateness

The amount and nature of an assessment discussion with students will obviously vary with their age. It is, however, important that students are involved with assessment at an early age. This will help them to develop an assessment vocabulary and also their ability to self-assess. Students who have an opportunity in the primary grades will have a sophisticated understanding of assessment in high school.

Age of students will influence the way in which information is shared with them. When most students in a class can read, it is not sufficient to simply tell students how they will be assessed; it is appropriate to provide assessment information in writing—to students and parents.

## Amount of Detail

Students must be able to manage and understand the details about assessment of a whole course or an individual assessment. Information, especially about how grades will be determined, needs to be clear and concise. Ideally, teachers use methods to calculate grades that are not complicated.

## The Beginning of Instruction

Involve students in discussion about assessment during the first week of classes. At about the same time that teachers review learning goals and course content, they also inform students about assessment. Timing is critical so that students see that assessment is integral, not just an add-on, to learning. This is equally important for the big picture—how assessment may be used throughout the course—as well as for the small picture—how assessment of each course aspect and each separate summative assessment will be done.

Ideally, teachers discuss assessment with students and provide a written assessment plan, including grading for each course, but these assessment plans are not carved in stone. If teachers believe a change is needed, they are flexible and make the change. It would be ideal to discuss the proposed change with students, but, at the very least, students must be informed of any change. This principle applies also to marking schemes or rubrics used to score assessments—if it becomes obvious during the scoring process that there is something wrong with the scoring approach, then the rubric is changed. Once again, students are informed about the why and what of the change, and the amended scoring approach is, of course, applied to the work of all students.

**Timing is critical so that students see that assessment is integral, not an add-on, to learning.**

## Test the Teaching, Don't Teach the Test

It almost goes without saying that when it comes to tests and exams, students must know what will be included. This knowledge covers the content of the test/exam as well as the types of questions and how the test/exam will be marked. As Schafer says

> tests and other assessments should not surprise students. They should be aware of (the learning goals) . . . and understand what they will be asked to do to provide evidence of their learning. This does not mean that teachers should "teach to the test" (at least in the traditional meaning of this phrase); it means that teachers must "test the teaching" in a way which is fair and reasonable for their students. (1997, 545)

# What's the Bottom Line?

Student involvement in developing assessment approaches and student understanding about how their academic achievement will be assessed, including how grades will be determined, is critical to support learning and encourage student success. Assessment is not something that is done to students separate and apart from instruction; assessment must be—and must be seen to be—something that is done with students, an integral part of the learning process.

# What's My Thinking Now?

Analyze Guideline 8 for grading (Discuss assessment, including grading, with students at the beginning of instruction) by focusing on three questions:

Why use it?

Why not use it?

Points of uncertainty

After careful thought about these points, answer these two questions:

Would I use Guideline 8 now?

Do I agree or disagree with the guideline, or am I unsure at this time?

(See the following for one person's reflections on Guideline 8.)

# A Reflection on Guideline 8

## WHY USE IT?

- expectations are clear to all
- students learn better
- student and parent buy-in is greater
- no secrets or mystery to grading
- stops any game playing, favoritism

## WHY NOT USE IT?

- student understanding of assessment is too limited
- puts teacher in a straitjacket—too restrictive
- sets up false idea that life is fair
- does not allow sufficiently for individual differences in students
- teacher should be in control

## POINTS OF UNCERTAINTY

- degree of student involvement?
- variation with student age/grade level?
- amount of time needed to do this effectively?
- amount of teacher collaboration needed?
- appeal mechanism?

# CHAPTER 9

# MORE GRADING ISSUES

The task of reforming educational assessment has just begun. New forms of assessment cannot provide clearer or more complete information about student achievement unless the ways in which achievement is communicated are replaced. The real challenge for assessment reform will be to bring assessment and grading practices into the fold.

— Cizek 1996, 103

There are many grading issues that have not been dealt with or are only touched upon in the detailed consideration of the grading guidelines. In this chapter, six issues will be examined: grading systems, grading exceptional students, computer grading programs, calculating grade point averages (GPAs), legal issues, and grading policies. Discussion focuses on raising the issues, providing some direction, and identifying references that have more detailed analyses.

# Grading Systems

There are a large number of grading systems in use in schools in North America. Some school districts use checklists or rating scales, especially when grading younger students. Pass/fail systems are used in some districts and colleges. The most common system is the use of letter grades, usually on a five point scale (A, B, C, D, F). Closely related are grading systems with numerical scores, usually percentages. There is a great debate about which of these systems is better—that is, has clear meaning and encourages learning.

## Checklists or Rating Scales

Many critics of grading favor the use of checklists or rating scales because they provide real rather than symbolic information. An advantage is that they focus on individual achievement rather than on comparison between students.

## Pass/Fail Systems

Some educators prefer the use of pass/fail or credit/no credit systems—they believe that all that is necessary or desirable is to identify whether students have reached the minimum level of achievement necessary to obtain credit and/or to move to the next level.

The very difficult issue that has to be resolved with both checklist and pass/fail systems is what constitutes the necessary minimum level of achievement—one would hope and expect that it would be rather different, for example, for a surgeon or a pilot than for a Grade 9 visual arts student.

## Letter Grades

Symbol systems using letters or numbers are the most commonly used grading systems. Letter grades may have three to five points on the scale.

> Many critics of grading favor the use of checklists or rating scales because they provide real rather than symbolic information.

Three point scales (e.g., Excellent, Satisfactory, Needs Improvement) are used most commonly for Grades 1, 2, and 3.

Four point scales are usually designed without a failing grade. Variations include (1) A, B, C, and Pass and (2) HP (High Pass), P (Pass), LP (Low Pass) and I (Incomplete). Those in favor of four point scales suggest that they improve student attitudes toward learning by producing less competition and less cheating, while developing more creativity and increased student self-esteem. Critics of four point scales contend that they are unrealistic and that they are really five point scales without the fifth point added.

Five point scales—A, B, C, D, F—are the most commonly used scales in the United States (see Figure Intro.4). Most school districts establish numerical equivalents for letter grades (most commonly, A: 90% to 100%, B: 80% to 89%, C: 70% to 79%, D: 60% to 69%, and F: less than 60%, but see also Introduction, Case Study 5), and some have detailed descriptors for the characteristics of each letter grade. (See for example, the policy of the Cupertino, California, Elementary School District in Robinson and Craver 1989, 113). As was indicated in the Introduction, opinions differ considerably about the value of this type of grading system.

**Grades are not precise and so should be reported as a range rather than as an exact number.**

## Numerical Scores

A similar debate occurs around the use of numerical scores. Many school districts, especially those in Canada, report grades as percentages, either as one number (e.g., 73%) or as a five percent grade range (e.g., 70% to 74%). Proponents of the latter approach argue that grades are not precise and so should be reported as a range rather than as an exact number.

## Precision: Real or Imagined?

Impreciseness is also the main point of those who argue for letter grades rather than percentage grades; they believe that dividing student achievement into a limited number of categories is all that we can ever hope to do with any pretense of real meaning. According to this argument, using a 100 point scale gives a false sense of precision and, therefore, detracts from the main purpose of grades—meaningful communication of student achievement.

This argument has a great deal of merit for elementary and middle schools, where grades are not involved in high stakes decisions, except

## Letter Versus Percentage Grades

| Subject | Jack | | Jacqueline | | English |
|---|---|---|---|---|---|
| | % | Letter | % | Letter | |
| English | 89 | B | 90 | A | Summative Assessment #1 |
| Mathematics | 89 | B | 90 | A | Summative Assessment #2 |
| Social Studies | 89 | B | 90 | A | Summative Assessment #3 |
| Science | 89 | B | 90 | A | Summative Assessment #4 |
| Computer Studies | 89 | B | 90 | A | Summative Assessment #5 |
| Music | 89 | B | 90 | A | Summative Assessment #6 |
| Total | 534 | | 540 | | |
| Mean | 89 | B | 90 | A | |

Figure 9.1

**The use of letter grades with percentage equivalents advantages some students while disadvantaging others.**

pass/fail. However, in any situation where grades are involved in high stakes decisions, that is, where they influence decisions about students' educational future, such as college entrance, graduate school acceptance, and employment opportunities, numbers are preferable to letters because there are more scale points available.

Figure 9.1 dramatically illustrates this problem. With letter grades, arbitrary cutoffs must be set; so, whether one is calculating a grade for a subject (right side) or for an overall grade average (left side), students who score just below the cutoff point are seriously disadvantaged relative to those whose scores are right on the cutoff point. In Figure 9.1, Jacqueline scored only 1% higher on each summative assessment and in each subject than Jack, but her English grade and her grade average were A's, whereas Jack received Bs. This is obviously an extreme example, but it illustrates very clearly that the use of letter grades with percentage equivalents advantages some students while disadvantaging others. This is not acceptable when students' futures are at stake.

If all the guidelines and principles described in Chapters 1 to 8 are applied, then letter grades based on teachers' professional judgments using

## Sample Descriptive Grading Criteria

Students receiving a grade demonstrate most of the characteristics most of the time.

**A**
- exhibits novel and creative ways to show learning
- enjoys the challenge and successfully completes open-ended tasks with high quality work
- test scores indicate a high level of understanding of concepts and skills
- assignments are complete, high quality, well organized, and show a high level of commitment
- almost all the learning goals are fully or consistently met and extended

**B**
- exhibits standard ways to show learning
- enjoys open-ended tasks, but needs support in dealing with ambiguity
- test scores indicate a good grasp of concepts and skills
- assignments are generally complete, thorough, and organized
- most of the learning goals are fully or consistently met

**C**
- needs some encouragement to show learning
- needs support to complete open-ended tasks
- test scores indicate satisfactory acquisition of skills and concepts
- assignments are generally complete, but quality, thoroughness, and organization vary
- more than half of the learning goals are fully or consistently met

**D**
- occasionally shows learning after considerable encouragement
- needs support to begin, let alone complete, open-ended tasks
- test scores indicate weak acquisition of skills and concepts
- assignments are very varied in quality, thoroughness, and organization
- only a few of the learning goals are fully or consistently met

**F**
- rarely shows learning
- unable to begin, let alone complete, open-ended tasks
- test scores indicate very weak grasp of concepts and skills
- assignments show poor quality and are frequently incomplete
- none or almost none of the learning goals are fully or consistently met

Adapted from original work by Sharon Anderson, Dave Layzell, and Bob Belcher.

Figure 9.2

**Further Reading**
Keefe 1984, 75–76
Madgic 1988, 29–34
Robinson and Craver 1989, 14–16

a detailed descriptive scale (see Figure 9.2 and Robinson and Craver 1989, 113) will produce the best grades. But if teachers crunch numbers to arrive at grades, especially in high school and college, then percentage grades are fairer, and therefore better, than letter grades.

# Grading Exceptional Students

This is one of the most difficult grading issues for teachers, especially in school districts that have explicit or implicit norm-referenced approaches to grading. It definitely is preferable not to grade specially challenged students using letter or numerical grades. Checklists or rating scales that focus on improvement or learning gain are more appropriate; but if district policy or parental expectations require traditional grades, remember that although each of the grading guidelines are relevant to this issue, pay primary attention to Guidelines 4 and 6 for exceptional students.

## Applying Guideline 4

Grading should always be related to learning goals. If these have been adapted to accommodate the needs/abilities of exceptional students, then grading should be based on the adapted goals, not those that apply to regular students. Reporting of grades based on adapted learning goals should clearly indicate that such adaptation has been made and ideally should indicate what the adaptations are.

## Applying Guideline 6

Grading should always be based on criterion-referenced standards, not norms. In a gifted class, if all student results meet the predetermined standard, then all should receive A's. If some students' performances are also well above that standard, this becomes a reporting variable, but it is not a grading variable. The bottom line here is that no student should be disadvantaged by being the weakest student in a high-achieving group, nor should any student be advantaged by being the strongest student in a low-achieving group.

For identified special education students, whether mainstreamed or not, the grades they receive should be based on the extent to which they meet the adapted predetermined standards. If they meet this standard, then they should get A's, and, as noted, reporting should clearly indicate that the standards have been changed from those that apply to nonidentified students.

The grades obtained by identified exceptional students based on adapted learning goals/standards should never be used to compare exceptional students with other students. However, as there is some evidence (Selby and Murphy 1992, 97) that identified exceptional students do not value

> It definitely is preferable not to grade specially challenged students using letter or numerical grades.

adapted grades, consideration could be given to reporting two grades for these students—the grade on the adapted goals and the grade that (probably) would have been reported if the grades/standards had not been adapted.

## Applying Other Guidelines

Teachers grading exceptional students may also consider other criteria:

- individual achievement (Guideline 1)
- summative assessments (Guideline 2)
- the most recent information (Guideline 3)
- the teacher's professional judgment, not just number crunching (Guideline 5).

If all of these practices are followed, exceptional students will receive grades that are meaningful and that support their learning. The key is that grades are based on public learning goals/standards and reflect real achievement, not some vague perception of their effort and their achievement relative to their ability.

# Computer Grading Programs

Stiggins said, "It troubles me deeply that so many 1990's teachers still maintain grade records the way teachers did at the turn of the century" (Stiggins 1997, 442).

## Why Use a Grading Program?

If teachers follow the guidelines discussed in this book, record keeping is a complex endeavor:

1. Achievement data needs to be separated from other information, such as effort and participation (Guideline 1).

2. Formative scores need to be separated from summative assessments (Guideline 2).

3. More recent information takes the place of older information, and second—or more—chance assessment scores need to be recorded (Guideline 3).

4. Grades are related to learning goals (Guideline 4).

5. Numerical calculations involve more than the mean, and weighting factors need to be applied consistently (Guideline 5).

**Further Reading**

Cohen 1983

Engelberg and Evans 1986

Hargis 1990

Munk and Bursuck 1997/98

Rojewski, Pollard, and Meers 1991

Selby and Murphy 1992

Whitton and Mowrer 1995

---

## A Sampling of Computer Grading Programs

| | | |
|---|---|---|
| eClass | Chancery Software Ltd., Barnaby, B.C. | 800-999-9931 |
| GrA⁺de Machine | Misty City Software, Seattle, WA | 425-820-5559 |
| Whaley Grading Program | Whaley Gradebook Co. Inc., Grand Junction, CO | 970-241-7777 |
| Micro Grade | Chariot Software Group, San Diego, CA | 619-298-0202 |

Note: This list is not intended as an endorsement. Phone numbers are current as of 1998.

Figure 9.3

---

Unless teachers rely completely on the most recent information and their professional judgment, this complexity means that most teachers will be doing at least some number crunching, which, whether done manually or by using a calculator, takes a great deal of time.

This wasted time may be reduced by using one of a variety of available grading software packages to more efficiently enter, calculate, store, retrieve, and summarize grading data. If teachers are very competent computer users, they may develop their own systems using spreadsheet programs. Figure 9.3 lists some software that was available in 1998. Inclusion on this list is not intended as endorsement of any product, but is simply information for teachers who may wish to investigate one or more of these products.

**The teacher must be able to control the program; the program should not control how the grades are determined.**

### Potential Problems

There is one major potential problem with computer grading programs that teachers need to be aware of—grading programs vary considerably in what they can and cannot do. Before deciding on a particular program, check that the program has the flexibility to calculate grades the way the teacher (you) wants. The teacher must be able to control the program; the program should not control how the grades are determined. In order to follow Guidelines 1, 2, and 3, the grading program would have to allow a nil value for data the teacher wants on file but does not want included in the grade, for example, formative assessment scores such as quizzes and first drafts.

Another problem that teachers must be aware of is "garbage in, garbage out," or put less colorfully—if incorrect information is entered into the computer, incorrect grades will be calculated. Teachers must check for errors in the same manner that they check manually calculated grades.

As long as these potential shortcomings are avoided, teachers are encouraged to use computer grading programs to save time, which the teacher can use more productively to help students.

## Beyond Grading Calculations

Also, be aware that software is available for a number of other assessment functions. These include collecting classroom observation records (e.g., Learner Profile), creating portfolios of student work (e.g., Grady Profile), developing classroom assessments, primarily in mathematics (e.g., Objective Tracker), and managing curriculum information (e.g., Digital Chisel). Again, the programs listed are not being endorsed but are offered as examples.

**Further Reading**
Brewer and Kallick 1996, 178–187
Kasnic 1995, 196–202
Mengeling 1996
Vockell and Kopenec 1989

# Calculating Grade Point Averages

Grade Point Averages (GPAs) are traditionally used by many schools to determine standing on the honor roll and class rank and, in some places, eligibility for cocurricular activities. Also, many colleges use GPAs as all or part of acceptance decisions. Thus, they are very important for students. How they are calculated is a matter of concern for school board members, administrators, and teachers.

## Mathematical Calculation Systems

### The Four Point Scale

Traditionally, grade point averages have been calculated over the four years of high school on the following basis: A, 4 points; B, 3; C, 2; D, 1; and F, 0.

### Weighted Scales

Some school districts use other approaches to calculating GPAs. Gilman and Swan (1989) identified seven different systems, all of which included sliding scales for A, A–, B+, B, B–, and so on. They say that "the most common system . . . is to assign different weights to some courses" (1989, 92–93). Weighting is applied to more difficult courses such as calculus and honors and advanced placement classes, so that for these courses a higher value is assigned to grades, for example, A = 5.2, A– = 4.77, B+ = 4.33, B = 3.9, and so on.

## Problems With GPA Systems

Weighting is done to overcome one of the most serious criticisms of GPAs, which is that unweighted systems encourage students to take easy courses to inflate their GPAs. Weighted GPAs are intended to encourage students to take the more difficult courses without penalizing them when they receive lower grades. In the example earlier, a student would get more points for a B+ on a weighted course than for an A on an unweighted course.

One of the major problems with weighted systems is that they cause problems between teachers who are teaching courses that are weighted and those who are teaching unweighted courses. Partly for this reason and partly because of community attachment to existing systems, it is often very difficult to change how GPAs are calculated. As an example, Ashenfelter (1990) described a two-year struggle in High School District 214, Illinois, in his wonderfully titled article "Our Schools Grappled with Grade Point Politics and Lost."

## Effect of Using GPAs

Even more basic than concern for the mathematical system used to calculate GPAs is the need for schools, school communities, and colleges to examine the whole GPA process and its effects. The first question that needs to be considered is what is the effect of the use of GPAs? Clearly, the main effect is to turn the whole high school experience into a four-year competition that emphasizes points rather than learning. This is obviously inconsistent with the philosophy expressed in this book—and the mission statements and goals of many school districts. Because very few colleges disadvantage students in admission decisions if they do not have class rank or GPA information, the necessity for this mathematical, noneducational process needs to be seriously debated.

If, however, after debating the issue of whether to calculate GPAs, a school district decides in favor of GPAs, then a second question needs to be considered—over how many years should a GPA be calculated? Students change quite dramatically over their high school years; very frequently, underachieving freshmen become high-achieving seniors. Why should their first year performance be held against them at the end of high school? Guideline 3 states that for grading decisions, we should use the most recent information. The same principle applies to GPA calculation—if GPAs are used, calculate them only on an annual basis and never

**What is the effect of the use of GPAs? The main effect is to turn the whole high school experience into a four-year competition that emphasizes points rather than learning.**

**Further Reading**
Ashenfelter 1990
Gilman and Swan 1989
Nemecek 1994

cumulatively. For college admission, the only GPA that should count is that of the senior year.

# Legal Issues

Teachers, especially in the United States, need to be aware that grading is, or can become, a legal minefield. Obviously, if this is a major personal concern, a lawyer should be consulted, but here are a few general comments on two aspects of grading that have attracted legal attention—lowering grades for nonacademic misconduct and due process, or the lack of it.

## Lowering Grades for Nonacademic Misconduct

Hobbs (1992) reported on several cases in which school officials were ordered to reinstate students' grades, which had been lowered because of students' absences, some of which were due to suspension. In these cases, the principle that the courts applied is that lowering grades as a disciplinary matter is illegal because it causes academic achievement to be misrepresented.

## Due Process

Hobbs noted, however, that "the courts do not always decide for the plaintiff in challenges to academic practices or policies that deal with student grades" (1992, 205). The key issue appears to be due process—if school officials have notified students of their rights and responsibilities, and if there is an appeal process within the school/school district, then the courts are much more likely to rule in favor of the school. If, on the other hand, actions taken by teachers/schools are seen as being arbitrary, capricious, or in bad faith, then the courts are willing to intervene and rule in favor of students who have been denied due process.

It appears that the legality of grades is established when academic and nonacademic factors are kept separate and when students are accorded due process. All the grading guidelines have a part to play in ensuring that grades can stand up to scrutiny by the courts. In particular, following Guidelines 1 and 8 should help teachers protect themselves against legal challenges to their grading practices.

> **U.S. courts have found that lowering grades as a disciplinary matter is illegal because it causes academic achievement to be misrepresented.**

**Further Reading**
Hobbs, 1992 and 1989
Phillips, 1997

# Grading Policy

District or school policies need to be in place so that teachers know what procedures to follow in their classrooms. Also, as indicated in the previous section, the existence of clearly stated grading policies helps protect educators from legal challenges to their grading practices.

The problem with most school and/or district policies is that they usually only establish what grades are, for example, A is 93% to 100%, B is 88% to 92%, and so on, but give very little guidance to teachers on what is to be included in grades and how they are to be calculated. This produces a lack of consistency between and within schools. When policies provide detail, it is usually a litany of rules for lowering grades in extremely punitive ways.

What is needed are grading policies and procedures that provide the basis for a reasonable level of consistency between and within schools and that provide specific guidance for teachers at the classroom/grade book level. Any such policies also support learning and encourage student success. These are the purposes for which the guidelines described in this book have been developed. The guidelines can be translated into policy language. A sample grading policy based on the guidelines is provided in Appendix 2.

**Further Reading**

Arter and Stiggins 1991

Earl and Cousins 1995

Manitoba Education and Training 1997

**CHAPTER 10**

# COMMUNICATING STUDENT ACHIEVEMENT TO OTHERS

*The report should paint a rich, accurate, and honest profile of*

*achievement, progress, and growth.*

—Wiggins (1996, 176)

The primary purpose of grades is to communicate meaningful information to students, parents, teachers, potential employers, colleges, and other individuals and institutions concerning the achievement status of students. Although grades will be meaningful and will support learning if they are developed following the guidelines described in this book, much more is needed to communicate effectively with all those who need quality information about student achievement. Whether they are letters or numbers, grades are merely symbols; in order to provide real information, they should be seen as only a part—probably a very small part—of our communication system.

All of the methods listed in the continuum shown in Figure 10.1 have a place in effective communication systems. The most effective communication, however, takes place when several methods are used and when these methods come increasingly from the right-hand side of the continuum.

**Grades are merely symbols and are only a part—probably a very small part—of our communication system.**

## Report Cards

Traditionally, report cards, especially for secondary schools, have been little more than a list of grades and brief comments about student progress and behavior. Because comments were severely limited in length, they were frequently of little value. Comments such as "a pleasure to teach" or "try for honors next term" do little to provide understanding of student achievement or directions for the future.

## Expanded Format Reporting

For report cards to provide effective communication, they need to have an expanded format in which information can be given on student achievement of specific learning goals and of general learning skills or work habits. In addition, other reporting opportunities are provided by expanded format reports, including

- sharing student achievement on cross-curricular or exit learning goals
- reflecting by students on their own strengths, weaknesses, and goals
- acknowledging actions that need to be taken by partners in learning—students, parents, and teachers
- writing an anecdotal summary comment on each student by teachers
- meeting legal requirements, such as attendance, lates, promotion status, and signatures.

| The Communication System Continuum | | | | | | | |
|---|---|---|---|---|---|---|---|
| Grades | Report Cards (limited information, usually grades and brief comments) | Informal Communications (infrequent, usually criticism/ warning) | Parent/Teacher Interviews (no student present) | Report Cards (expanded format) | Informal Communication (frequent and ongoing, usually positive) | Student-Involved Conferencing | Student-Led Conferencing |

Figure 10.1

Expanded format report cards provide a great deal of information, but what is provided must not overwhelm parents. Two sides of 8½″ x 14″ paper is a sufficient size; parents do not need, want, or benefit from a small book! Equally important is that what is expected must not overwhelm teachers; the reporting workload must not require so much time that teachers are virtually unable to teach in the week(s) just before report card time. Also, the number of formal reports per year must be reasonable; two or three expanded format report cards are sufficient as long as other means of communication, described later, are also used.

Figure 10.2 is a sample of an expanded format report card, prepared on two-sided 8½″ x 14″ paper. It is used twice a year (January and June) and is supported by informal communications, by a much briefer interim report in late October/early November, and by student-involved conferencing in late November and mid-April. It is emphasized that this report card is presented not as a model, but rather as an example that demonstrates some of the desirable characteristics of expanded format reporting.

The report card in Figure 10.2 provides 70 to 80 pieces of information on each student, of which only 7 or 8 are grades. Thus, grades are provided for those parents (and others) for whom grades are important, but a much richer and broader picture of each student is provided by the other information. Anyone receiving an expanded format report of this type can really appreciate the complexity of the learning process and the achievement of the student.

The learning goal statements on this report come from a menu produced by the school district central office in consultation with classroom teachers. There are two main advantages to this shared menu approach. First,

**What is provided must not overwhelm parents. What is expected must not overwhelm teachers.**

# Progress Report

STUDENT NUMBER:
GRADE:

STUDENT:                    DATE:                    PROGRAM
TEACHER:                    PRINCIPAL:               ATTACHMENTS

| | ESL/ESD | SPECIAL ED. | SPEC. ED. RES. |
|---|---|---|---|
| PROGRAM ATTACHMENTS | | | |

*Student achievement is measured by comparison to program outcomes.*

| **E** | EXTENDING THE OUTCOME | **I** | IMPROVING BUT NOT YET MEETING THE OUTCOME |
|---|---|---|---|
| **M** | MEETING THE OUTCOME | **N** | NOT YET MEETING THE OUTCOME |

| SUBJECT | MARK RANGE | EXPECTED OUTCOMES | COMPLETES ASSIGNMENTS | PARTICIPATES IN CLASS | USES CLASS TIME WISELY |
|---|---|---|---|---|---|
| ENGLISH | 75–79 | ( M ) knows and uses the rules and patterns of the English language<br>( M ) uses written and spoken English language in different situations and for different purposes<br>( M ) uses language to think and learn collaboratively and independently<br>( M ) demonstrates attitudes that promote language learning | M | M | M |
| MATHEMATICS | 75–79 | ( M ) demonstrates proficiency in calculations involving whole numbers, decimals, and fractions and applications of order of operations with paper and pencil<br>( M ) solves problems with simple equations using formal methods or systematic trial<br>( M ) recognizes and describes situations where a particular graph should be used<br>( M ) develops and applies strategies to solve variety of problems | M | M | M |
| FRENCH | 65–69 | ( M ) interprets spoken French and communicates intelligibly with peers and teacher<br>( M ) accurately pronounces the vocabulary and expressions presented this term<br>( I ) shows a knowledge of the agreement of adjectives with their respective nouns<br>( E ) has a knowledge of the basic verbal forms and can apply them in sentences<br>( E ) shows a positive and responsible attitude toward learnng French | E | M | E |
| GEOGRAPHY | 80–84 | ( E ) uses appropriate geographic vocabulary<br>( M ) gathers, organizes, and records information from a variety of sources<br>( M ) demonstrates cooperative learning skills<br>( E ) communicates effectively by means of pictures, symbols, maps, and/or graphs | E | M | E |
| HISTORY | 75–79 | ( M ) identifies and describes the contributions of men and women that have shaped Canada's identity<br>( M ) understands that history is defined and driven by change<br>( M ) understands the way in which Canada is connected to the rest of the world | M | M | M |
| SCIENCE | 90–94 | ( E ) organizes and reports data in a variety of ways<br>( E ) makes and records observations accurately<br>( M ) uses appropriate scientific vocabulary when sharing information and expressing ideas<br>( E ) accepts responsibility for learning as an individual and in team situations | E | M | E |

| SUBJECT | EXPECTED OUTCOMES | COMPLETES ASSIGNMENTS | PARTICIPATES IN CLASS | USES CLASS TIME WISELY |
|---|---|---|---|---|
| DESIGN/TECHNOLOGY FAMILY STUDIES | ( E ) demonstrates safe working habits and practices<br>( M ) works cooperatively with others<br>( M ) creates a product to specific guidelines<br>( M ) identifies family dynamics, responsibilities, and roles | M | M | M |
| MUSIC | ( M ) derives enjoyment and enrichment through participating in the performing, listening, and creating of music (function)<br>( I ) applies learned skills through performance (communication) | M | M | M |
| VISUAL ARTS | ( M ) used many ways to solve problems<br>( E ) demonstrates a positive attitude toward creating and appreciating art | M | M | M |
| PHYSICAL EDUCATION | ( E ) participates actively and safely in a balanced instructional program of daily physical activities<br>( M ) develops and maintains a level of physical fitness appropriate for active living | E | E | M |
| HEALTH EDUCATION | ( M ) performs well in all areas/aspects of the program | M | M | M |

Figure 10.2a

SkyLight Training and Publishing Inc

# Progress Report

## CROSS-CURRICULUM REPORTING STATEMENTS

| E | EXTENDING THE OUTCOME | MC | MEETING THE OUTCOME CONSISTENTLY | MI | MEETING THE OUTCOME INCONSISTENTLY | N | NOT YET MEETING THE OUTCOME | NR | NOT REPORTING |
|---|---|---|---|---|---|---|---|---|---|

| | | | |
|---|---|---|---|
| **MC** uses appropriate technology to enhance learning | | **MI** applies problem-solving strategies |
| **MC** accesses resources in the school and community | | **MC** initiates and completes learning tasks |
| **MC** applies information processing strategies | | **MC** uses reflection to enhance learning |
| **E** reads/views/listens for personal growth and enjoyment | | **MC** makes personal meaning of information and shares knowledge |

## PERSONAL DEVELOPMENT AND SOCIAL RESPONSIBILITY

| **C** CONSISTENTLY | **S** SOMETIMES | **R** RARELY |
|---|---|---|

| | |
|---|---|
| **C** contributes constructively to the classroom, school, and community | **R** participates willingly in cooperative group tasks |
| **S** practices environmental responsibility | **S** negotiates conflicts peacefully |
| **C** demonstrates respectful behavior | **C** makes responsible decisions |
| **C** empathizes with others | _____ |

## STUDENT SELF REFLECTION (STRENGTHS, CONCERNS, GOALS)

_____ STUDENT'S NAME Please Print     _____ CLASS     _____ STUDENT'S SIGNATURE

### TEACHER COMMENTS

TEACHER'S SIGNATURE

## RECOMMENDED ACTIONS

☐ NO SPECIFIC RECOMMENDATIONS AT THIS TIME

| STUDENT | PARENT/GUARDIAN | TEACHER |
|---|---|---|
| ☐ Participate in extracurricular activities | ☐ Encourage student to seek help | ☐ Provide extra help |
| ☐ Continue an interest in _____ | ☐ Read with your child daily | ☐ Contact support services |
| ☐ Work on appropriate behavior | ☐ Reinforce appropriate behavior | ☐ Reinforce appropriate behavior |
| ☐ Improve attendance | ☐ Ensure regular attendance | ☐ Provide ongoing communication |
| ☐ _____ | ☐ _____ | ☐ _____ |

## ATTENDANCE/PUNCTUALITY

Total absence this school year is _____ day(s), as of _____
Times Late: _____                                    PRINCIPAL'S SIGNATURE

## PLACEMENT IN SEPTEMBER (June only)

Placement: _____

## TO PARENTS OR GUARDIANS AND STUDENTS

Figure 10.2b

SkyLight Training and Publishing Inc

it takes advantage of computer technology (specifically FileMaker Pro), and so the reporting task is easier and less time consuming for teachers. Second, it provides quality control. Although there is no doubt that the best report is a well-written anecdotal report, all teachers are not able to write high quality reports, especially by the time they get to students 32, 33, and 34 in a 34-student class. Reporting statements that are based on published learning goals prevent comments like "Joanie is a nice girl and we studied dinosaurs." Also, if teachers know that they have to report using these type of statements, their assessment and teaching tends to be based more strongly on the learning goals. Teaching and assessment alignment thus occurs naturally as a result of the pressure and support provided by the reporting system.

## Informal Communications

This is another aspect of planning for schools—seeking to ensure that each parent receives at least one positive informal communication each term.

Brief meetings in the school, phone calls, postcards, and quick notes are all informal communications that teachers use. Although informal, they are part of the communication system. If communication is seen as a system, even informal communications are planned, at least to some extent. Planning involves the availability of postcards or quick notes so that it is easy for teachers to send informal written communications home. If using printed cards or notes that have a set format, teachers have only to fill in the blanks and the communication is ready to go.

Although schools have always seen it as their duty to inform parents when students misbehave or are frequently tardy or absent, it is important that informal communication be used also for positive feedback. This is another aspect of planning for schools—seeking to ensure that each parent receives at least one positive informal communication each term. For this to happen, teachers need to keep brief records of their use of informal communications. Informal communication and the associated record keeping must not be a major burden for teachers; as with other methods of communication, planning is needed to ensure that teacher workload is reasonable. In addition, teachers need flexibilty in choosing a method that is most comfortable for them—some prefer to make phone calls, others, to write.

## Student-Involved Conferencing

A third part of a communication system involves planned meetings between parents, teachers and, increasingly, students. Traditionally, these

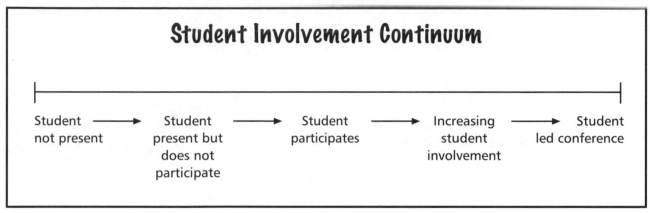

Figure 10.3

meetings have been parent-teacher interviews with no student participation. Much valuable information can be exchanged in such interviews, and although sometimes privacy is necessary, almost always parents, teachers, or both discuss the interview with students afterwards. How much better if the student is actually present and participates in the conference rather than receives second-hand, and inevitably somewhat distorted, accounts of what occured. This leads to the concept of student-involved conferencing.

The continuum shown in Figure 10.3 demonstrates that forms of student-involved conferencing vary from those in which the student is merely present as a listener but not really participating through increasing student participation to conferences that are truly led by students. Schools and teachers may start at the point on the continuum that is comfortable for them and their community. There is a huge variety of possible formats, and it is hoped that teachers will move quickly toward increasing levels of student involvement.

**Schools and teachers may start at the point on the continuum that is comfortable for them and their community.**

In one possible format, students share work samples that demonstrate their growth and their best work with their parent(s). Students identify for their parent(s) the strengths and weaknesses of the shared samples and what they could do to improve on a similar task in the future. Work samples may come from an organized portfolio assessment system, but it is not essential to have student portfolios to institute student-involved conferencing. Teachers can simply state the number of pieces of work that students are to share, some designated by the teacher and some chosen by the students. This approach applies particularly to interviews for middle and high school students (see Figure 10.4), where parents have many teachers to see and teachers have very limited amounts of time with each student and his or her parent(s).

---

## Parents' Night Interview - Science

Dear _____,

I look forward to meeting you on Thursday, _____ at _____ p.m. in Room
_____. Your daughter/son is welcome to attend, too.

Before you come to see me, please find time to sit down with your daughter/son and ask
her/him to show you the following from her/his SCIENCE NOTEBOOK:

1. Two pieces of work that she/he is particularly pleased with
2. One piece of work that she/he could have done better on
3. The self-tracking sheet outlining progress on the essential performance criteria
4. The self and teacher evaluation of her/his participation in the learning process

Please discuss these pieces of work with her/him. I suggest you make several positive
comments and outline one or two steps for improvement if necessary. Please bring this
sheet with you on parents' night.

Positive comments:


Steps for improvement:


Questions arising from your discussion:


Many thanks,
[Signature]

Adapted by permission from Hillary Gerrard, Assistant Head of Science, Thornlea, S.S. York Region
District School Board, Ontario, Canada.

Figure 10.4

Students may lead conferences in the absence or presence of teachers.
One of the most practical formats is to have a number of conferences
occurring at the same time—the number largely determined by the size of
the available room. Students lead each conference by taking their
parent(s) through each work sample and inviting their reactions to the
work and the student's description and explanation. The teacher deals
with any problems that arise and spends a relatively short period of time
with each student and parent(s). For example, conferences may be set for

45 minutes, with 4 to 8 different student-parent groups meeting simultaneously and with the teacher rotating among the groups, giving about 5 minutes to each, a mix of what Davies, Cameron, Politano, and Gregory (1992) call two-way and three-way conferences.

As with other parts of the communication system, student-involved conferencing requires a great deal of preparation and planning. Students have to be trained for whatever type of involvement they are to have, and parents need to be informed about how conferencing will be conducted and what is expected of them. Millar Grant, Heffler, and Meriwether (1995, 51) provided a detailed, generic, four-month calendar, which includes all the steps teachers need to prepare a class for student-involved conferencing.

Student-involved conferencing has many benefits for students, parents, and teachers. Students hone their self-assessment abilities and develop their understanding and vocabulary about learning and assessment. They also learn in a very powerful way that they are responsible for their own learning.

Parents are able to see their children as learners and gain a much richer understanding of their student's growth and progress than is provided by report cards. Often, in fact, where student-involved conferencing is used, report cards play a very small part in the conference because the real information is in the shared work samples. Parents who speak only a language other than the first language of the school benefit greatly from this approach because very often the student conducts the conference in the parents' first language.

Teachers benefit from student-involved conferencing by improved communication with and between students, parents, and teachers, which develops a better understanding of their students' strengths and weaknesses and, thus, promotes dealing with them more effectively. Another major benefit for teachers (and schools) is that attendance by parents at student-involved conferences is almost always much better than at traditional parent interviews.

It is hard to think of any major problems with student-involved conferencing apart from logistical/time issues. It is obviously much easier to organize conferences for a self-contained Grade 2 class than it is for a Grade 8 class or a high school on a rotary timetable but, as indicated earlier, there are ways to adapt this approach for all grade levels. For

**Student-involved conferencing has many benefits for students, parents, and teachers.**

example, universities have been using a version of student-involved conferencing (without parents) for centuries. They do this by having students attend lectures in large groups, but then organizing students into small tutorial groups where students meet with a leader (often a graduate student) to examine their understanding of the concepts and problems presented by the professor in the lecture.

One small problem: student-involved conferencing does mean that teachers lose some of the control that they have with parent/teacher interviews. As with other aspects of communication, teachers search to find a comfort zone in which they honor the principle (in this case, student involvement) to the extent that it is comfortable for them. Some teachers want to begin with the type of conference in which the students are just present, whereas others are happy to jump right in to student-led conferencing. The important thing is that teachers involve students, and over time, move further to the right of the continuum (Figure 10.3). At all times, parents should be offered the opportunity for a parent/teacher interview in place of, or in addition to, a student-involved conference.

## Summary

Schools and teachers have a responsibility to communicate effectively with parents and others who are interested in the progress of students. Traditionally, report cards with letter or percentage grades and brief comments have been the main vehicles for communication. This has led to cult-like status for grades, but grades are only part of the communication system. In addition to, or where acceptable, in place of, these symbols, teachers can provide parents with real information by using expanded format reporting, informal communications, and student-involved conferencing. School districts, schools, and teachers must plan their communication system carefully and train students, parents, and teachers to participate effectively in the system. Prime considerations in developing such systems are effective and clear communication and reasonable work loads for teachers. This is not a situation where more is always better; careful choices need to be made that are within the comfort zone of both teachers and the community and that move everyone involved toward more effective communication.

**Schools and teachers have a responsibility to communicate effectively with parents and others who are interested in the progress of students.**

**CHAPTER 11**

# THE WAY AHEAD

*The time has come to* de-emphasize traditional grades *and to* demystify the entire grading process. *We need to* focus *instead on the* process of learning *and the* progress of the individual student.

(Burke 1993, viii)

This may seem an odd quote to start the final chapter of a book on grading, but it does summarize the intent and message of this book. Let us look at this by discussing each of the main ideas.

## De-Emphasizing Traditional Grades

Traditional grades have both too little and too much meaning. They have too little meaning because there are so many things mixed in them, in such idiosyncratic ways by different teachers, that their meaning is very unclear. They have too much meaning because of the cult-like status accorded them and because of their importance in high stakes educational decisions. Traditional grades may be de-emphasized: (1) by new approaches to grading, which provide grades with clear meaning; and (2) by giving to students, parents, and interested others information about learning that is much better than grades.

## New Approach to Grading

The grading guidelines described and analyzed in this book produce grades with meaning, that is, grades that are based on individual achievement data (Guideline 1), that use the most recent information (Guideline 3), that are derived from summative assessments (Guideline 2), and that are based on opportunities for reassessment (Guideline 3). These grades are directly related to learning goals (Guideline 4) and result from appropriate number crunching, if necessary (Guideline 5). They are derived from quality assessments (Guideline 7), that are based on public, criterion-referenced standards (Guideline 6) and have been thoroughly discussed with and understood by students (Guideline 8).

As a result of all these characteristics, this new approach to grading supports learning and encourages student success. This contrasts markedly with traditional grades, which have little to do with learning because they are competitive, punitive, and encourage game playing by students and teachers alike. Traditional grades encourage grade grubbing, not learning, and are often used just as control measures. Grading with the guidelines de-emphasizes and differs from traditional grades (see Figure 11.1).

## Information About Learning That Is Much Better Than Grades

Portfolios, expanded format reporting, effective informal communication, and student-involved conferencing each provide better information than

**Traditional grades encourage grade grubbing, not learning, and are often used just as control measures.**

## New Grading Contrasted With Traditional Grading

| Guideline | New | Traditional |
|---|---|---|
| 1 | individual achievement only | uncertain mix of achievement, attitude, effort, and behavior; often includes group marks |
| 2 | from summative assessments only | from formative and summative assessments |
| 3 | most recent information only | everything marked is included |
| | reassessment without penalty | multiple assessments recorded as average, not best |
| 4 | directly related to learning goals | usually related to assessment methods |
| 5 | limited, careful number crunching | many formulas and calculations |
| | some use of medians | always use means ("average") |
| 6 | criterion-referenced standards | often norm-referenced or a mix of criterion and norm |
| | public criteria/targets | criteria unclear or assumed to be known |
| 7 | derived from quality assessments | huge variation in assessment quality |
| | data carefully recorded | often only stored in teachers' heads |
| 8 | all aspects discussed with students | teacher decides and announces |

Figure 11.1

grades. Grades are—and can never be anything more than—symbols that summarize achievement. These methods provide real information about student learning far more effectively than grades because each contains a wealth of information and provides an effective method to communicate the information.

Educators (and the media) have a responsibility to educate parents and the community about the place of grades in the communication system. In the past, this frequently has not been done well. An unfortunate example of this is provided by the province of Ontario, which introduced a standard Provincial Report Card for Grades 1 to 8 beginning in the 1997 to 1998 school year. Although many school districts in Ontario (including the author's) did not previously provide grades on report cards given to students in Grades 1 to 6, the new Provincial Report Card required the use of letter grades for Grades 1 to 6 and percentage grades for Grades 7 and 8. These grades were required not for clearly justified educational reasons, but because, according to the politicians, "this is what parents said they wanted." It is hoped that elementary educators in Ontario—and elsewhere—will be able to prevent a fixation on grades in the early years by providing parents with other methods of communication, ones that give a fuller picture of their children as learners.

A hopeful sign at the other end of the educational spectrum is that many colleges and universities are increasingly requiring information in addition to or in place of grades. They recognize that to make good selection decisions about students, they need more information than is provided by grades, GPA, and/or class rank. Supplementary information forms, which provide students with the opportunity to present themselves as a whole person, are being used by many postsecondary institutions.

## Demystifying the Entire Grading Process

For the most part, grading has been the preserve of individual teachers operating in the isolation of their own classrooms with minimal direction from school or district policies and minimal guidance from administrators. The grading guidelines presented in this book demystify the process in several ways:

1. Guideline 8 requires that students be part of the process that establishes grading procedures. If they are not part of the process, at the very least, they must be well informed about assessment and grading procedures.

2. If these guidelines are adopted, it is expected that they will be given policy status at both the school and district level. This means that grading procedures are no longer a mystery and teachers can be held accountable for the procedures they follow. A grading policy based on the guidelines is provided in Appendix 2.

3. In many ways, grading has also been a mystery for teachers because there is so little discussion about grading in education courses, staff development and conference workshops, or staff rooms. Teachers

> **Grading has been the preserve of individual teachers operating in the isolation of their own classrooms with minimal direction.**

have basically done what was done to them or relied on individual help from a more experienced colleague. These grading guidelines demystify the process for teachers because they provide a clear, practical process for teachers to follow in their classrooms—and in their grade books.

# Focusing on the Process of Learning

Although grades always ultimately focus on the results of learning, use of the grading guidelines, expanded format reporting, and the other methods of communication advocated in this book honors the process of learning far more than traditional grading. Guidelines 2 and 3, in particular, acknowledge learning as a process:

1. They require that formative assessment provides reporting, not grading, information.

2. They emphasize that summative assessment is the only proper source of information for grades.

3. They emphasize the most recent information rather than early information or first attempts.

4. They provide two or more assessment opportunities.

Seeing grades as only part of the communication system and emphasizing other methods of communication that provide more detailed information also moves the focus more to the process of learning.

# Focusing on the Progress of the Individual Student

There are many ways in which the guidelines focus on the individual student. First and foremost, Guideline 1 emphasizes individual achievement; although it is critically important that teachers use cooperative learning structures in their classrooms, it is even more important that any marks that students get from cooperative learning activities, either process or product, be based on each individual's contribution, not the achievement, or lack of achievement, of others. Group grades are totally inappropriate and should not be used because they are so unfair and because they contribute in a significant and unfortunate way to giving cooperative learning a bad reputation.

Another way in which these guidelines focus on the individual student is that they acknowledge students as individuals and enable individuals to

> **Teachers have basically done what was done to them or relied on individual help from a more experienced colleague.**

progress because their learning styles, multiple intelligences profile, and/or needs are taken into account. Guideline 3 acknowledges that students learn at different rates and need varying amounts of time to be able to adequately demonstrate their knowledge and skills. Guideline 5 suggests using medians rather than means, which to allows students to have a few stumbles without the poorer performances detracting from their normal level of achievement. Guideline 6 leads to each individual student having the opportunity to succeed at the highest level. Criterion-referenced standards foster learning that is not a competition and prevents success from being artificially rationed because of a mathematical formula. Guideline 7 requires that teachers record assessment data accurately and consistently—producing quality information to provide to students and parents about the progress of each individual student. Guideline 8 gives every individual the best opportunities to progress because it requires that students be involved in, and clearly understand, how assessment and grading will be carried out. Finally, this information is provided in ways that can contribute to the growth of individuals, because as grades are seen as only part of the communication system, other methods of communication that give rich information about the strengths and weaknesses of each student are used. This rich information enables students to be effective self-assessors and assists them, their parents, and their teachers to set goals and to identify needed actions to reach those goals.

> The prime purpose of grades is recognized as communication, not competition.

## Summary

Using the grading guidelines and the communication methods described in this book is a new—or at least a different—approach to grading and reporting. The guidelines and methods go a long way toward providing the student-centered assessment advocated by Stiggins (1997) and the honesty and fairness in grading and reporting that Wiggins (1996) has been advocating for many years. They also clearly acknowledge that grading and reporting must be directly related to learning goals and standards, which have become such a large part of education (Marzano and Kendall 1996). This approach to grading and communication does what Burke advocated—"de-emphasize traditional grades," "demystify the entire grading process," and "focus on the process of learning and the progress of the individual student" (Burke 1993, viii). All of these desirable characteristics occur because the prime purpose of grades is recognized as communication, not competition, and because the orientation of teachers is that every step along the way to student grades is based on a pedagogy that views the teacher's role as supporting learning and encouraging student success.

# Recommendations

Although the focus of this book is grading, it is important to acknowledge that there are many things more important than grading in education, especially quality instruction and assessment. There are many steps that teachers must take to implement the grading guidelines advocated in this book. They require a philosophy and a whole assessment approach that include the following six action steps (only one of which is grading itself!), adapted from Midwood, O'Connor, and Simpson:

1. Use a variety of assessment methods so that the needs of all students can be addressed.

2. Match assessment methods with learning goals and/or purposes; generally, this will require more use of performance assessment and clearer identification of formative assessment.

3. With student involvement (where appropriate), develop clear criteria (rubrics) and provide models (exemplars or anchor papers) illustrating the levels of performance. Base marking on these criteria and levels.

4. Provide reteaching and reassessment opportunities.

5. Encourage assessment by self and peers—this could include the use of portfolios, response journals, and student-involved conferencing

6. Base grades on only the most recent, summative, individual achievement data. (1993, 401)

**There are many things more important than grading in education.**

# What's My Thinking Now?

Having now reached this point in the book (and, it is hoped, having read all of it!), readers are in a position to consider two things—how the ideas presented will influence their own practices and what the links are between the grading guidelines. With this in mind, two final activities are provided.

First Activity: This activity asks teachers to examine their own grading practices and consider changes that will benefit their students. Readers are encouraged to answer the questions and share the results with a colleague.

1. Which grading practices were reinforced by the book?
2. What revisions to my grading practices do I need to make?
3. What points of uncertainty still exist?
4. What actions do I want to take now?

Second Activity: This activity begins a web of the grading guidelines; readers are encouraged to complete the web by identifying the links between the grading guidelines and the links to the ideas and issues discussed in Chapters 9 and 10.

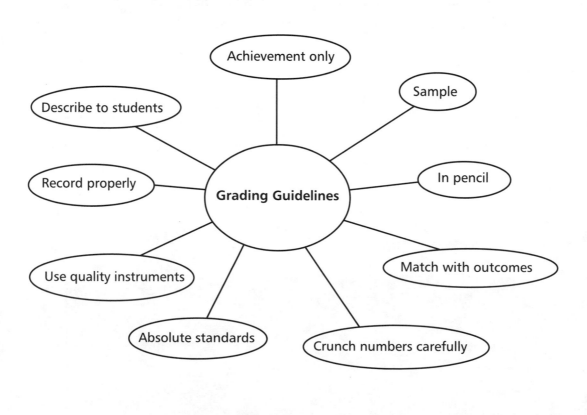

APPENDIX 1

# Glossary

The glossary is an explanation of the way terms are used in this book. It is based on many sources, but the major source is the glossary developed by the Evaluation Policy Committee of the Scarborough Board of Education, Ontario, Canada.

**achievement.** The demonstration of student performance measured against learning goals/objectives.

**assessment.** Gathering and interpreting information about a student or group of students, using a variety of tools and techniques. It is the act of describing student performance, primarily for the purpose of enhancing learning.

**criteria.** Characteristics or dimensions of student performance.

**criterion-referenced.** Assessment of students' success in meeting stated objectives, learning goals, expectations, or criteria. (See also *norm-referenced* and *self-referenced*.)

**diagnostic.** Assessment/evaluation carried out prior to instruction that is designed to determine a student's attitude, skills, or knowledge in order to identify specific student needs. (See also *formative* and *summative*.)

**evaluation.** Making judgments about the quality of overall student performance, primarily for the purpose of communicating student achievement.

**formative.** Assessment designed to provide direction for improvement and/or adjustment to a program for individual students or for a whole class, that is, quizzes, initial drafts/attempts, homework, and questions during instruction. (See also *diagnostic* and *summative*.)

**grade.** The number or letter reported at the end of a period of time as a summary statement of student performance. (See also *mark*.)

**learning goal.** An observable result demonstrated by a student's knowledge, skills, or behavior.

**mark.** The number or letter "score" given to a student on any single test or performance. (See also *grade.*)

**norm referenced.** Assessment/evaluation in relation to other students within a class or across classes/schools or a segment of the population. (See also *criterion-referenced* and *self-referenced.*)

**reliability.** The consistency with that an assessment strategy measures whatever it measures. (See also *validity.*)

**rubric.** A set of guidelines for assessment which states the characteristics and/or the dimensions being assessed with clear performance criteria and a rating scale.

**self-referenced.** Assessment designed to compare an individual's performance with his or her previous performance. (See also *criterion-referenced* and *norm-referenced.*)

**summative.** Assessment/evaluation designed to provide information to be used in making judgments about a student's achievement at the end of a period of instruction, that is, tests, exams, final drafts/attempts, assignments, projects, performances. (See also *diagnostic* and *formative.*)

**standard.** Description of the expected level of performance.

**validity.** The degree to which an assessment strategy measures what it is intended to measure. (See also *reliability.*)

APPENDIX 2

# A Proposed Grading Policy

If the ideas and guidelines presented in this book were to be included in a school or district grading policy, the wording should be similar to the following (the number of each section parallels the grading guidelines):

1. a. Individual achievement of stated learning goals shall be the only basis for grades.
   b. Effort, participation, attitude, and other behaviors shall not be included in grades but shall be reported separately unless they are a stated part of a learning goal.
   c. Late work
      (1) Teachers shall set due dates and absolute deadlines for all marked work that will be part of a student grade.
      (2) Work handed in late shall be penalized at no more than 2% per day to a maximum of 10%.
      (3) Teachers may exempt students from penalties, if any are applied, in exceptional circumstances.
   d. Absence
      (1) Students shall not be penalized only for absence.
      (2) Absent students shall be given make-up opportunities for all missed summative evaluations (marked work that will be part of student grades) without penalty.
2. a. Teachers shall mark and/or provide feedback on formative assessment.
   b. Marks for formative assessment shall not be included in grades.
   c. Marks from summative assessments only shall be included in grades.
3. a. Where repetitive measures are made of the same or similar knowledge, skills, or behaviors, the most recent mark or marks shall replace the previous marks for grade calculations.
   b. Second chance (or more) assessment opportunities shall be made available to students; students shall receive the highest, most consistent mark, not an average mark for any such multiple opportunities.
4. Grading procedures shall be related directly to stated learning goals.
5. a. Grades shall be calculated to ensure that the grade each student receives is a fair reflection of his or her performance.
   b. Consideration shall be given to the use of statistical measures other than the mean for grade calculations, for example, consider using medians.
   c. Grades shall be weighted carefully to ensure the intended importance is given to each learning goal and to each assessment.
6. Criterion-referenced standards shall be used to distribute grades and marks.
7. a. Teachers shall use quality assessment instruments.
   b. Teachers shall properly record evidence of student achievement on an ongoing basis.
8. a. Teachers shall discuss assessment with students, in an age appropriate manner, at the beginning of instruction. Where feasible, students shall be involved in decisions about methods of assessment and scoring scales.
   b. Teachers shall provide to students and parents a written overview of assessment, including grading, in clear, easily understandable language during the first week of classes in each course or grade.
   c. Teachers shall provide students with a written overview in clear, easily understandable language, indicating how each summative assessment throughout the course will be evaluated before each such assessment is administered.

APPENDIX 3

# References

Anderson, K. E., and F. C. Wendel. 1988. Pain relief: Make consistency the cornerstone of your policy on grading. *The American School Board Journal*, October, 36–37.

Airasian, P. W. 1994. *Classroom assessment.* 2d. ed. New York: McGraw-Hill.

Armstrong, T. 1994. *Multiple intelligences in the classroom.* Alexandria, Va.: Association for Supervision and Curriculum Development.

Arter, J., and R. Stiggins. 1991. *Assessment policy: Workshop notes.* Portland, Oreg.: NorthWest Regional Educational Laboratory.

Ashenfelter, J. W. 1990. Our schools grappled with grade point politics and lost. *The Executive Educator*, January, 21–23.

Bailey, J., and J. McTighe. 1996. Reporting achievement at the secondary level: What and how. In *Communicating student learning: ASCD yearbook 1996,* edited by T. R. Guskey. Alexandria, Va.: Association for Supervision and Curriculum Development.

Baron, M. A., and F. Boschee. 1995. *Authentic assessment: The key to unlocking student success.* Lancaster, Pa.: Technomic.

Bellanca, J. 1992. How to grade (if you must). In *If minds matter: A foreword to the future*, Vol. 2, edited by A. L. Costa, J. Bellanca, and R. Fogarty. Palatine, Ill.: Skylight Publishing.

Bonstingl, J. J. 1992. *Schools of quality: An introduction to total quality management in education.* Alexandria, Va.: Association for Supervision and Curriculum Developoment.

Brewer, W. R., and B. Kallick. 1996. Technology's promise for reporting student learning. In *Communicating student learning: The ASCD yearbook 1996*, edited by T. Guskey. Alexandria, Va.: Association for Supervision and Curriculum Development.

Brookhart, S. M. 1994. Teacher's grading: Theory and practice. *Applied Measurement in Education* 7(4): 279–301.

Burke, K. A. 1993. *The mindful school: How to assess authentic learning.* Palatine, Ill.: IRI/Skylight Publishing.

Burke, K. A., R. Fogarty, and S. Belgrad. 1994. *The mindful school: The portfolio connection.* Palatine, Ill.: IRI/Skylight Publishing.

Busick, K. U., and R. J. Stiggins. 1997. *Making connections: Case studies for student-centered classroom assessment.* Portland, Oreg.: Assessment Training Institute.

Canady, R. L., and P. R. Hotchkiss. 1989. It's a good score: Just a bad grade. *Phi Delta Kappan*, September, 68–71.

Chapman, C. 1993. *If the shoe fits . . .: How to develop multiple intelligences in the classroom.* Palatine, Ill.: IRI/Skylight Publishing.

Cizek, G. J. 1996a. Grades: The final frontier in assessment reform. *NASSP Bulletin*, December, 103–110.

———. 1996b. Setting passing scores. *Educational Measurement: Issues and Practices*, summer, 20–31.

Cohen, S. B. 1983. Assigning report card grades to the mainstreamed child. *Teaching Exceptional Children*, winter, 86–89.

Costa, A. L., and B. Kallick. 1992. Reassessing assessment. In *If minds matter: A foreword to the future*, Vol. 2, edited by A. L. Costa, J. Bellanca, and R. Fogarty. Palatine, Ill.: Skylight Publishing.

Culp, L., and V. Malone. 1992. Peer scores for group work. *Science Scope*, March, 35, 36, 59.

Danielson, C. 1997. *A collection of performance tasks and rubrics: Upper elementary school mathematics.* Larchmount, N.Y.: Eye on Education.

Darling-Hammond, L., R. Ancess, and B. Falk.

1995. *Authentic assessment in action.* New York: Teachers College Press.

Davies, A., C. Cameron, C. Politano, and K. Gregory. 1992. *Together is better: Collaborative assessment, evaluation and reporting.* Winnipeg, MB, Canada: Peguis Publishing.

Earl, L., and J. B. Cousins. 1995. *Classroom assessment: Changing the face, facing the change.* Toronto, ON, Canada: Ontario Public School Teachers Federation.

Ebert, C. 1992. So when can I take the retest? *Quality Outcomes-Driven Education*, December, 32–34.

Engelberg, R. A., and E. D. Evans. 1986. Perceptions and attitudes about school grading practices among intellectually gifted, learning disabled and normal elementary school pupils. *Journal of Special Education*, Spring, 91–101.

Fogarty, R., and J. Bellanca. 1987. *Patterns for thinking: Patterns for transfer.* Palatine, Ill.: Skylight Publishing.

Frary, R. J., L. M. Gross, and L. J. Weber. 1992. Testing and grading practices and opinions in the Nineties: 1890's or 1990's. Paper presented at the Annual Meeting of the National Council on Measurement in Education, April 21–23, at San Francisco, Califorinia.

Frisbie, D. A., and K. K. Waltman. 1992. Developing a personal grading plan. *Educational Issues: Measurement and Practice*, fall, 35–42.

Gardner, H. 1983. *Frames of mind: The theory of multiple intelligences.* New York: HarperCollins.

Gilman, D. A., and E. Swan. 1989. Solving G.P.A. and class rank problems. *NASSP Bulletin*, March, 91–97.

Glasser, W. 1990. *The quality school.* New York: Harper Perennial.

Grading performance assessments. 1996. *ASCD Education Update*, December, 4–5.

Gregory, K., C. Cameron, and A. Davies. 1997. *Knowing what counts: Setting and using criteria.* Merville, B.C., Canada: Connections Publishing.

Gronlund, N. E., and R. L. Linn. 1990. *Measurement and evaluation in teaching.* 6th ed. New York: Macmillan.

Guskey, T. R. 1993. *ASCD Update.* September, 7.

———. 1994. Making the grade: What benefits students? *Educational Leadership*, October, 14–20.

———. 1996. Reporting on student learning: Lessons from the past—prescriptions for the future. In *Communicating student learning: The ASCD yearbook 1996*, edited by T. R. Guskey. Alexandria, Va.: Association for Supervision and Curriculum Development.

Hargis, C. H. 1990. *Grades and grading practices: Obstacles to improving education and to helping at-risk students.* Springfield, Ill.: Charles C. Thomas.

Harlen, W., and M. James. 1997. Assessment and learning: Differences and relationships between formative and summative assessments. *Assessment in Education: Principles, Policy and Practices*, November, 365–379.

Hart, G. 1996. Grades: Both a cause and result of fear. *Middle School Journal*, March, 59–60.

Hensley, L. D., R. Aten, T. A. Baumgartner, W. B. East, L. T. Lambert, and J. L. Stillwell. 1989. A survey of grading practices in public school physical education. *Journal of Research and Development in Education* 22(4): 37–42.

Hills, J. R. 1991. Apathy concerning grading and testing. *Phi Delta Kappan*, March, 540–545.

Hobbs, G. J. 1989. The issuance of student grades and the courts. Paper presented to the Annual Meeting of the Eastern Educational Research Association, February 22–25, at Savannah, Georgia.

———. 1992. The legality of reducing student grades as a disciplinary measure. *The Clearing House*, March/April, 204–205.

Johnson, B. 1996. *The performance assessment handbook.* Vol. 1, *Portfolios and socratic seminars.* Princeton, N.J.: Eye on Education.

Juarez, T. 1990. Revitalizing teacher planning—Grade eggs, not learners. *Holistic Education Review*, winter, 36–39

———. 1996. Why any grades at all, Father? *Phi Delta Kappan*, January, 374–377.

Kagan, S. 1994. *Cooperative learning.* San Clemente, Calif.: Kagan Cooperative Learning.

———. 1995. Group grades miss the mark. *Educational Leadership*, May, 68–71.

Kain, D. L. 1996. Looking beneath the surface:

Teacher collaboration through the lens of grading practices. *Teachers College Record,* summer, 569–587.

Kasnic, M. 1995. Expanding reporting options through technology. In *Report card on report cards: Alternatives to consider,* edited by T. Azwell and E. Schmar. Portmouth, N.H.: Heinemann.

Keefe, J. W. 1984. Assessing and reporting student progress. In *Instructional leadership handbook,* edited by J. W. Keefe and J. M. Jenkins. Reston, Va.: National Asssociation of Secondary School Principals.

Kirschenbaum, H., R. Napier, and S. B. Simon. 1971. *Wad-ja-get?: The grading game in American education.* New York: Hart Publishing.

Kohn, A. 1991. Group grade grubbing vs. cooperative learning. *Educational Leadership,* February, 83–87.

———. 1993a. Choices for children: Why and how to let students decide. *Phi Delta Kappan,* September, 9–19.

———. 1993b. *Punished by rewards: The trouble with gold stars, incentive plans, A's, praise and other bribes.* New York: Houghton Mifflin.

Linek, W. M. 1991. Grading and evaluation techniques for whole language teachers. *Language Arts,* February, 125–132.

MacIver, D. J., and D. A. Reuman. 1993/94. Giving their best—Grading and recognition practices that motivate students to work hard. *American Educator,* winter, 24–31.

Madgic, R. F. 1988. The point system of grading; A critical appraisal. *NASSP Bulletin,* April, 29–34.

Mahon, R. L. 1996. A grading system for composition papers. *The Clearing House,* May/June, 280–282.

Malehorn, H. 1994. Ten measures better than grading. *The Clearing House,* July/August, 323–324.

Manitoba Education and Training. 1997. *Reporting on student progress and achievement.* Winnipeg, MB, Canada: Manitoba Ministry of Education and Training.

Manon, J. R. 1995. The mathematics test: A new role for an old friend. *Mathematics Teacher,* February, 138–141.

Marzano, R., and J. S. Kendall. 1996. *A comprehensive guide to designing standards-based districts, schools, and classrooms.* Aurora, Col.: MidContinent Regional Education Laboratory/Association for Supervision and Curriculum Development.

Matanin, M., and D. Tannehill. 1994. Assessment and grading in physical education. *Journal of Teaching in Physical Education* 13: 395–401.

McTighe, J. 1996/97. What happens between assessments. *Educational Leadership,* December/January, 6–12.

McTighe, J., and S. Ferrara. 1995. Assessing learning in the classroom. *Journal of Quality Learning,* December, 11–27.

Mengeling, M. A. 1996. *Computer software for classroom assessment.* Portland, Oreg.: Assessment Training Institute.

Midwood, D., K. O'Connor, and M. Simpson. 1993. *Assess for success.* Toronto, ON, Canada: Ontario Secondary Teachers Federation.

Millar Grant, J., B. Heffler, and K. Meriwether. 1995. *Student-led conferences.* Markham, ON, Canada: Pembroke.

Munk, D. D., and W. D. Bursuck. 1997/98. Can grades be helpful and fair? *Educational Leadership,* December/January, 44–47.

National Association of Secondary School Principals. 1996. *Breaking ranks: Changing an American institution.* Reston, Va.: National Association of Secondary School Principals.

Nemecek, P. M. 1994. Constructing weighted grading systems. *The Clearing House,* July/August, 325–326.

Nottingham, M. 1988. Grading practices—Watching out for land mines. *NASSP Bulletin,* April, 24–28.

O'Connor, K. 1995. Guidelines for grading that support learning and student success. *NASSP Bulletin,* May, 91–101.

Olson, L. 1995. Cards on the table. *Education Week,* June 14.

Phillips, S. E. 1997. Standards and grading for disabled students. *National Council on Measurement in Education Quarterly Newsletter,* May, 2.

Pomperaug Regional School District 15. 1996. *A teacher's guide to performance-based learning and assessment.* Alexandria, Va.: Association for Supervision and Curriculum Development.

Pratt, D. 1980. *Curriculum design and development.* New York: Harcourt Brace Jovanovich.

Reedy, R. 1995. Formative and summative assessment: A possible alternative to the grading-reporting dilemma. *NASSP Bulletin*, October, 47–51.

Regional Educational Laboratories. 1998. *Improving classroom assessment—A toolkit for professional developers—Toolkit 98.* Washington, DC: U.S. Department of Education, Office of Educational Research and Improvement.

Robinson, G. E., and J. E. Craver. 1989. *Assessing and grading student achievement.* Arlington, Va.: Educational Research Service.

Rogers, S., and S. Graham. 1997. *The high performance toolbox.* Evergreen, Col.: Peak Learning Systems.

Rojewski, J. W., R. R. Pollard, and G. D. Meers. 1991. Grading mainstreamed special needs students: Determining practices and attitudes of secondary vocational educators using a qualitative approach. *Remedial and Special Education*, January/February, 7–15, 28.

Schafer, W. D. 1997. Classroom assessment. In *Handbook of academic learning,* edited by G. D. Phye. San Diego, Calif.: Academic Press.

Seeley, M. 1994. The mismatch between assessment and grading. *Educational Leadership,* October, 4–6.

Selby, D., and S. Murphy. 1992. Graded or degraded: Perceptions of letter grading for mainstreamed learning disabled students. *British Columbia Journal of Special Education* 16(1): 92–104.

Sheeran, T. J. 1994. Measuring and evaluating student learning in cooperative settings: Practices, options and alternatives. *Social Science Record*, spring, 20–24.

Spady, W. G. 1987. On grades, grading and school reform. *Outcomes*, winter, 7–12.

———. 1991. Shifting the grading paradigm that pervades education. *Outcomes*, spring, 39–45.

Sperling, D. 1993. What's worth an "A"? Setting standards together. *Educational Leadership,* February, 73–75.

Spiegel, C. 1991. Grading schemes that reward students. *The Mathematics Teacher*, November, 631.

Stiggins, R. J. 1997. *Student-centered classroom assessment.* 2d ed. Upper Saddle River, N.J.: Merrill/Prentice Hall.

Stiggins, R. J., D. A. Frisbie, and P. A. Griswold. 1989. Inside high school grading practices: Building a research agenda. *Educational Measurement: Issues and Practices*, summer, 5–13.

Stiggins, R. J., and T. Knight. 1997. *But are they really learning?* Portland, Oreg.: Assessment Training Institute.

Terwilliger, J. S. 1989. Classroom standard setting and grading practices. *Educational Measurement: Issues and Practices*, summer, 15–19.

Thayer, J. D. 1991. Use of observed, true and scale variability in combining student scores in grading. Paper presented at the Annual Meeting of the National Council on Measurement on Education, April 4–6, at Chicago, Illinois.

Travis, J. 1996. Meaningful assessment. *The Clearing House*, May/June, 308–312.

Vockell, E. L., and D. Kopenec. 1989. Record keeping without tears: Electronic gradebook programs. *The Clearing House*, April, 355–359.

Whitton, L., and K. Mowrer. 1995. Making the grade: Assessing mainstreamed students in regular classes. *The High School Magazine*, June, 18–20.

Wiggins, G. 1996. Honesty and fairness: Toward better grades and reporting. In *Communicating student learning: The ASCD yearbook 1996,* edited by T. R. Guskey. Arlington, Va.: Association for Supervision and Curriculum Development.

Willis, S. 1993. Are letter grades obsolete? *ASCD Update,* September, 1, 4, 8.

Wright, R. G. 1994. Success for all: The median is the key. *Phi Delta Kappan*, May, 723–725.

APPENDIX 4

# Additional Resources

## Print Resources

Aker, D. 1995. *Hitting the mark: Assessment tools for teachers.* Markham, Ont., Canada: Pembroke.

Allison, E., and S. J. Friedman. 1995. Reforming report cards. *The Executive Educator,* January, 38–39.

Arnold, C. B., S. H. Reynolds, C. D. Stellern, D. Bohannon, K. Harmon, L. Hill, C. Mamantov, and S. Reed. 1992. Grading. *The Mathematics Teacher,* September, 442–443.

Azwell, T., and E. Schmar, eds. 1995. *Report card on report cards: Alternatives to consider.* Portsmouth, N.H.: Heinemann.

Bateman, C. F. 1988. Goldy's coffee. *Phi Delta Kappan,* November, 252–254.

Beckerman, L. 1996. Worth their while. *Executive Educator,* July, 31, 32, 39.

Berliner, D., and U. Casanova. 1998. Are grades undermining motivation? *Instructor,* October, 18–19.

Blackmore, L., and C. Politano. 1992–93. Half a dozen ways to make reporting powerful and painless. *Prime Areas* 35(3): 2.

Blynt, R. A. 1992. The sticking place: Another look at grades and grading. *English Journal,* October, 66–71.

Brandt, R. 1995. Punished by rewards: A conversation with Alfie Kohn. *Educational Leadership,* September, 252–254.

British Columbia Ministry of Education. 1994. *Guidelines for student reporting for the kindergarten to grade 12 education plan.* Victoria, B.C., Canada: Province of British Columbia, Ministry of Education.

Buckley, G. 1995. First steps: Redesigning elementary report cards. In *Report card on report cards: Alternatives to consider,* edited by T. Azwell and E. Schmar. Portsmouth, N.H.: Heinemann.

Bursh, P., and M. Neill. 1996. Principles to guide student assessment. *Thrust for Educational Achievement,* May/June, 16–19.

Bursuck, W., E. A. Polloway, L. Plante, M. H. Epstein, M. Jayanthi, and J. McConeghy. 1996. Report card grading and adaptations: A national survey of classroom practices. *Exceptional Children,* February, 301–318.

Cizek, G. J., R. E. Rachor, and S. Fitzgerald. 1995. Further investigation of teachers' assessment practices. Paper presented at the Annual Meeting of the American Educational Research Association, April 18–22 at San Francisco, California.

Clarridge, P. B., and E. M. Whitaker. 1994. Implementing a new elementary progress report. *Educational Leadership,* October, 7–9.

Collins, C. 1994. Grading practices that increase teacher effectiveness. *The Clearing House,* December, 167–169.

Curren, R. R. 1995. Coercion and the ethics of grading and testing. *Educational Theory,* fall, 425–449.

Foundation for Critical Thinking. 1996. *Critical thinking workshop handbook.* Santa Rosa, Calif.: Foundation for Critical Thinking.

Friedman, S. J., and M. Manley. 1992. Improving high school grading practices: "Experts" vs. "practitioners." *NASSP Bulletin,* May, 100–104.

———. 1998. Grading teachers' grading policies. *NASSP Bulletin,* April, 77–78.

Gaustad, J. 1996. *Assessment and evaluation in the multi-age classroom.* Eugene, Oreg.: Oregon School Study Council.

Gentile, J. R., and N. C. Murnyack. 1989. How shall students be graded in discipline-based art education? *Art Education,* November, 33–41.

Goodrich, H. 1996/97. Understanding rubrics. *Educational Leadership,* December/January, 14–17.

Gribbin, A. 1992. Making exceptions when grading and the perils it poses. *Journalism Educator,* winter, 73–76.

Haley, B. 1988. Does an A really equal learning? *NASSP Bulletin,* April, 35–41.

Herman, J. L., P. R. Aschbacher, and L. Winters. 1992. *A practical guide to alternative assessment.* Alexandria, Va.: Association for Supervision and Curriculum Development.

Johnson, B. 1996. *The performance assessment handbook.* Vol. 2, *Performances and exhibitions.* Princeton, N.J.: Eye on Education.

Jones, L. H., Jr. 1995. Recipe for assessment: How Arty cooked his goose while grading art. *Art Education,* March, 12–17.

Jongsmaa, K. S. 1991. Rethinking grading practices. *The Reading Teacher,* December, 318–320.

Juarez, T. 1994. Mastery grading to serve student learning in the middle grades. *Middle School Journal,* September, 37–41.

Kagan, S. 1996. Avoiding the group grades trap. *Learning,* January/February, 56–58.

Kenney, E., and S. Perry. 1994. Talking with parents about performance-based report cards. *Educational Leadership,* October, 24–27.

Kohn, A. 1994. Grading: The issue is not how but why. *Educational Leadership,* October, 38–41

Kulm, G. 1994. *Mathematics assessment—What works in the classroom.* San Francisco: Jossey-Bass.

Laska, J. A., and T. Juarez, eds. 1992. *Grading and marking in American schools.* Springfield, Ill.: Charles C. Thomas.

Lawton, V. 1994. Stressed-out students play numbers game. *Toronto Star,* April 23.

Lohman, D. F. 1993. Learning and the nature of educational measurement. *NASSP Bulletin,* October, 41–53.

Loyd, B. H., and D. E. Loyd. 1997. Kindergarten through grade 12 standards: A philosophy of grading. In *Handbook of academic learning, construction of knowledge,* edited by G. D. Phye. San Diego, Calif.: Academic Press.

Marzano, R., D. Pickering, and J. McTighe. 1993. *Assessing student outcomes: Performance assessment using the dimensions of learning model.* Alexandria, Va.: Association for Supervision and Curriculum Development.

Mazzarella, D. 1997. When everyone gets an A, grades are meaningless. *USA Today,* March 25.

Mehring, T., C. Parks, K. Walter, and A. Banikowski. 1991. Report cards: What do they mean during the elementary school years? *Reading Improvement,* fall, 162–168.

Nava, F. J. G., and B. A. Loyd. 1992. An investigation of achievement and nonachievement criteria in elementary and secondary school grading. Paper presented at the Annual Meeting of the American Educational Research Association, April 20–24, in San Francisco, California.

Noam, G., moderator. 1996. Assessment at the crossroads: A conversation. *Harvard Educational Review* 66(3): 631–657.

Nott, R. L., C. Reeve, and R. Reeve. 1992. Scoring rubrics: An assessment option. *Science Scope,* March, 44–45.

O'Connor, K. 1996. Grading—Myth, mystery or magic. *Research Speaks to Teachers,* April.

Ohlhausen, M. M., R. R. Powell, and B. S. Reitz. 1994. Parents' views of traditional and alternative report cards. *The School Community Journal,* spring/summer, 81–97.

O'Neil, J. 1994. Making assessment meaningful. *ASCD Update,* August, 1, 4, 5.

Ornstein, A. C. 1989. The nature of grading. *The Clearing House,* April, 365–369.

Rogers, E. 1994. Meeting student needs through the levels program and grade weighting. *The Clearing House,* July/August, 327–330.

Ryan, J. M., and J. R. Miyasaka. 1995. Current practices in testing and assessment: What is driving the changes? *NASSP Bulletin,* October, 1–10.

Selleri, P., F. Carugati, and E. Scappini. 1995. What marks should I give? *European Journal of Psychology in Education* 10(1): 25–40.

Shedlin, A., Jr. 1988. How about a national report card month. *Principal,* May, 34.

Sizer, T. 1996. *Horace's hope: What works for the American high school.* New York: Houghton Mifflin.

Stallings-Roberts, V. 1992. Subjective grading. *The Mathematics Teacher,* November, 677–679.

Stiggins, R. J. 1990. *Developing sound grading practices (Classroom Assessment Training).* Portland, Oreg.: Northwest Regional Educational Laboratory.

Thomas, W. C. 1996. Grading—Why are school policies necessary? What are the issues? *NASSP Bulletin*, February, 23–26.

Trotter, A. 1990. What to do if you're worried about how students are graded. *The Executive Educator,* January, 24–25.

Wiggins, G. 1991. Standards, not standardization: Evoking quality student work. *Educational Leadership,* February, 18–25.

———. 1994. Toward better report cards. *Educational Leadership*, October, 28–37.

Wilson, L. 1994. What gets graded is what gets valued. *The Mathematics Teacher,* September, 412–414.

Wilson, R. J. 1992. Evaluation of student achievement: Perception vs. reality. *Canadian School Executive,* April, 13–16.

———. 1994. Back to basics: A revisionist model of classroom-based assessment. Invited Presidential address to the Annual Meeting of the Canadian Educational Researchers Association, June, at Calgary, Canada.

——— 1996. *Assessing students in classrooms and schools.* Scarborough, Ont., Canada: Allyn & Bacon.

Wood, A. 1994. An unintended impact of one grading practice. *Urban Education,* July, 188–201.

Wright, R. G. 1989. Don't be a mean teacher. *Science Teacher,* January, 38–41.

Zeidner, M. 1992. Key facets of classroom grading: A comparison of teacher and student perspectives. *Contemporary Educational Psychology,* July, 224–243.

### Videos

Davies, A., and R. Stiggins. 1996. *Student-involved conferences.* Portland, Oreg.: Assessment Training Institute.

North Central Regional Educational Laboratory. 1991. *Schools that work: The research advantage, Volume 4.* Oak Brook, Ill.: North Central Regional Educational Laboratory.

Stiggins, R. 1995. *Creating sound classroom assessments.* Portland, Oreg.: Assessment Training Institute.

———. 1996. *Maximizing achievement in paper and pencil assessments.* Portland, Oreg.: Assessment Training Institute.

———. 1996. *Assessing reasoning in the classroom.* Portland, Oreg.: Assessment Training Institute.

Victoria Learning Society. 1992. *Observation: Finding the inner eye.* Victoria, B.C., Canada: Victoria Learning Society.

Wiggins, G. 1991. *Standards not standardization, Volumes 1– 4.* Geneseo, N.Y.: Center on Learning, Assessment, and School Structure.

### Association for Supervision and Curriculum Development Audiotapes

Guskey, T. R. 1996. *New news on grading, reporting and communicating student learning.* ASCD catalog number 96 3216.

Kohn, A. 1995. *From degrading to de-grading: Basic questions about assessment and learning.* ASCD catalog number 95 128.

Rogers, S. 1992. *Tackling the complex grading issues related to outcomes-based restructuring.* ASCD catalog number 92 6817.

### Internet Resources

Note: An annotated list of alternative assessment web sites can be found in "Finding Alternative Assessment Resources on the Web," by P. Butts, *Technology Connection,* December, 1997, 10–13.

Assessment Training Institute
http://www.assessmentinst.com/

Center on Learning, Assessment, and School Structure (CLASS)
http://www.classnj.org/

ERIC Clearinghouse on Assessment and Evaluation
http://ericae.net/

Kathy Schrock's Guide for Educators
http://www.capecod.net/schrockguide/

Michigan Electronic Library
http://mel.lib.mi.us/education/edu-assess.html

Midcontinent Regional Educational Laboratory.
http://www.mcrel.org/

National Center for Research on Evaluation,
Standards and Student Testing.
http://www.cse.ucla.edu/

North Central Regional Educational Laboratory
http://www.ncrel.org/

Northwest Regional Educational Laboratory
http://www.nwrel.org/

Southeastern Region Vision for Education
http://www.serve.org/

# Index

SkyLight Training and Publishing Inc

There are

one-story intellects,

two-story intellects, and three-story

intellects with skylights. All fact collectors, who

have no aim beyond their facts, are one-story men. Two-story men

compare, reason, generalize, using the labors of the fact collectors as

well as their own. Three-story men idealize, imagine,

predict—their best illumination comes from

above, through the skylight.

—*Oliver Wendell*

*Holmes*

# SkyLight

## PROFESSIONAL DEVELOPMENT

# We Prepare Your Teachers Today for the Classrooms of Tomorrow

*Learn from Our Books and from Our Authors!*

## Ignite Learning in Your School or District.

SkyLight's team of classroom-experienced consultants can help you foster systemic change for increased student achievement.

**Professional development is a process not an event.** SkyLight's experienced practitioners drive the creation of our on-site professional development programs, graduate courses, research-based publications, interactive video courses, teacher-friendly training materials, and online resources—call SkyLight Professional Development today.

**SkyLight specializes in three professional development areas.**

**Specialty #  1**

### Best Practices

We **model** the best practices that result in improved student performance and guided applications.

**Specialty #  2**

### Making the Innovations Last

We help set up **support** systems that make innovations part of everyday practice in the long-term systemic improvement of your school or district.

**Specialty #  3**

### How to Assess the Results

We prepare your school leaders to encourage and **assess** teacher growth, **measure** student achievement, and **evaluate** program success.

*Contact the SkyLight team and begin a process toward long-term results.*

2626 S. Clearbrook Dr., Arlington Heights, IL 60005
800-348-4474 • 847-290-6600 • FAX 847-290-6609
info@skylightedu.com • www.skylightedu.com